CW00688219

THE PROBLEM OF EVIL

(A study of evil, fate, freewill and predestination, forgiveness, and love)

RUQAIYYAH WARIS MAQSOOD

ADAM PUBLISHERS & DISTRIBUTORS
DELHI

ALL RIGHTS RESERVED

ADAM PUBLISHERS & DISTRIBUTORS
Exporters & Importers
Shandar Market, Chitli Qabar, Delhi - 110006
Phone (O) : 3271690, 3282550
Fax　　　　: 3267510 (R) 91- 4553953
e-mail:apd@bol.net.in
www.adampublishers.com

First Edition 2000

I S B N : - **81-7435-175-2**

Price :

Laser Typesetting by :
D. M. Computer Designer & Composer
Delhi-10

Printed & Bound in India :
Published by :
S. SAJID ALI for
ADAM PUBLISHERS & DISTRIBUTORS
Shandar Market, Chitli Qabar, Delhi-110006

'Those who patiently persevere and seek God with regular prayers and give generously, these overcome Evil with Good.'

(Surah 13:22)

CONTENTS

CHAPTER ONE

WHY DOES EVIL EXIST?

THE PROBLEM EXPRESSED

Anyone who wishes to believe in a God who is not only supposed to be Compassionate and Merciful, but also responsible for the world, is faced with a difficult problem. Nasty and painful things happen in our world. If God is supposed to be the Supreme Power, capable of doing absolutely anything He wishes, how come He allows these misfortunes to happen, if He is also supposed to be the Supreme Force for Good? How could an all-Powerful God be reconciled with a God of Love?

Now, if God is All-Powerful, then He must be able to do anything and everything; and if He is all-Good, then He cannot wish to see pain and suffering and evil in the world. Yet evil and suffering undoubtedly do exist - so this must mean that either God is powerless to stop them, (in which case He is not All-Powerful), or He is not aware that they are happening, (in which case He is not All-Knowing), or He doesn't care if they happen (in which case He is not All-Loving or All-Good). Clearly, if God can do anything, and yet in fact produces a cosmos in which there is suffering and evil, then there must be something wrong with His intentions. Conversely, if He is good, and there is nothing wrong with His intentions, and yet He produces an environment in which there is evil and suffering, then there must be something deficient in His power. Both conclusions are repugnant to Muslim doctrine, as they are also to Christian and Jewish doctrine that preceded the Muslim.

The faith revealed to all three Peoples of the Book is that God is both supremely good and is indeed the source of all values, and also that God created the universe out of nothing - a doctrine that emphasizes God's omnipotence. Other theological systems accepted that their gods were limited by the existing properties of matter and could only impose form on it without being able to rid it of chaotic tendencies. As far as Islam is concerned, Allah created the matter as well as the forms into which it became moulded.

Any person noticing the appalling effects of natural disaster, and the dreadful things that humans do to each other, must wonder why God doesn't do something about them. To those with ears to hear, the world resounds with desperate cries for help. We must wonder why these terrible sufferings exist at all. If God created everything, for what possible reason did He create evil? If He knows everything, He must know how unhappy it makes His people, so why didn't He stop it in the past, and why doesn't He stop it now? It is not just that God allows His created beings to behave badly, cause suffering, and err in the most cruel fashions, but also that the created cosmos inflicts on us the terrors and miseries of flood, famine, earthquake, tornado, pestilence and disease. Admittedly, some diseases and economic ruins are due to our own waywardness, but the vast majority of miseries are produced by the physical world, which is so often hostile to us, and to other living creatures. Everyday and everywhere unseen bitter strife and painful illness and a fight for survival are the lot of living creatures.

A human father who loves his children does not inflict suffering upon them gratuitously. Yet, if God is truly the Creator, He does.

Is God to Blame?

One is faced with the difficulty of explaining how there seems to be something limited about either God's power or His good intentions. Let's take a simple example. Suppose a nurse saw a man on a bed dying because he could not reach his medicine, and did not help him by handing it to him. Would we not then say that this heartless nurse had caused his death? A human being in those circumstances would certainly be charged with manslaughter, if not murder! So, how can we defend God, who sees and knows absolutely everything, and does nothing to help?

We could argue, I suppose, that God does not have the physical attributes of hands or speech, so how could He intervene? Whenever we talk of God 'seeing' everything, or of our souls being 'in His hands', we do not really mean that God has the physical attributes of hands or eyes, or any other part of the human anatomy. We have not the slightest idea of what God looks like, if He looks like anything at all. He exists beyond our knowledge and awareness, and even to say 'He' is a nonsense - just a habit when using human language. We could argue that God has two vehicles for helping, and they are already in use - our conscience and our sense of shame. He puts thoughts into our minds. It is we ourselves who should feel guilty when a man is dying alone, or, for that matter, when a nation's children are starving or being bombed.

That, of course, is little consolation to the poor chap dying on his own, if no-one comes to help him. Why doesn't God do more? What about the 'supernatural' powers? Couldn't God send a telepathic message to somehow who could then arrive in the nick of time and help the helpless man? Or, if the man prayed hard enough, couldn't God see to it that his pills miraculously rose up and floated across the room to him?

As a matter of fact, a study of newspaper articles following dreadful tragedies often reveals that some people do have premonitions or visions of things that later come to pass. Sometimes people feel these warnings so strongly that they act on them, and refuse to travel in the doomed plane or train. A New Testament example is the story of St Joseph (the husband of the Virgin Mary), who was warned in a dream of King Herod's evil intentions towards the infant Jesus ﷺ, and acted promptly by escaping with him to Egypt. We would love to know whether Joseph sent urgent messages round Bethlehem the night of his escape, desperately trying to warn other people with babies, and whether they just laughed at him - as disbelievers tend to do.

Herod killed the babies; and trains and planes crash. God does not intervene to save them by tampering physically in the human situation or with the Laws of Nature.

Naturally, we would like to sit back and cry 'Help!', and expect some sort of miraculous

intervention. Some people claim that the revealed
scriptures are full of stories of God's helpful and
miraculous interference on behalf of certain
individuals; this is true up to a point - but the
revealed texts are also full of outraged Hebrews and
later Muslim heroes (including, notably, the Prophet
🌸 himself) being laughed at by their enemies
because God had not rescued them from their
predicaments.

Christians, who believe the Blessed Jesus 🌸 to
be part of a Triune Godhead, God's own Son, base
their doctrine of salvation on the belief that God did
not even rescue Jesus from crucifixion. According
to the Gospels, Jesus 🌸 died surrounded by people
jeering and mocking him, and in spite of his agonised
cry 'My God! My God! Why have You forsaken
me? (St. Mark's Gospel 15:29-35). Naturally, all
people who expect miracles from Above to get them
out of sticky situations have the problem of finding
reasons why God does not help. They need face-
saving explanations.

Many Muslims, in their earnest devotion, insist
that if you have enough faith in Allah, then He will
take care of you and your problems, and everything
will come right for you. The simple devotion is
admirable, but it is not backed up by the facts.
Nobody was made to suffer more in abuse, ridicule,

torture and death than the Companions of the Prophet ﷺ, and the Prophet ﷺ himself. For every case where the Companions were able to claim Allah's help and salvation from their predicament, there are many outnumbering cases where the desired help was not forthcoming at all.

On the contrary, those early Muslims, as well as today's Muslims when they think about it honestly, have to accept that their loyalty and devotion to Allah might well lead to their suffering and even death in His cause. The main point for them (as for Jesus) ﷺ was 'not my will but Thine be done', even if meant that God required their death. Why such sacrifice? Obviously, the firm belief that the death of the human body is not the end of the story.

CHAPTER TWO

CLASSICAL SOLUTIONS TO THE PROBLEM

Islam has its own explanations for the origin of evil, the reasons for it, and the correct ways of facing it and dealing with it in this world. These were all revealed by Allah in the Holy Qur'an.

However, before we study these matters, we should take a look at some of the many other explanations that have been put forward over the centuries, and consider in what ways they are adequate or inadequate answers to the problem. A series of possible explanations are briefly outlined in this chapter.

1.   THERE IS NO GOD.

Of course, there is one very simple way out of the problem. It is to presume that the whole thing is complete nonsense, because God simply doesn't exist. There is no God. If there is no God, suffering and pain don't have to be explained away - they just have to be accepted as unfortunate facts of life. However, if we believe in a good and powerful God, then we are bound to ask why these evils exist? God must be responsible for them, ultimately if not directly, and that needs some explaining!

2. GOD EXISTS, BUT HIS POWER IS LIMITED

Assuming that God does exist, maybe we are wrong in our suppositions about Him. Suppose God does exist, but there is a limit to His power. In spite of our pious beliefs, there might be certain things which are beyond His control. Or maybe, He does control everything, but chooses to limit Himself according to His own Laws of Nature, by not intervening. Or how about this logical conundrum - If God can do absolutely everything, could He create a rock that was too heavy for Him to lift?

The Qur'an, the word of Allah, goes against all these possibilities. It states that there is no limit to the power of Allah:-

'God has power over all things.' (Surah 4:85)

'All things in the heavens and on earth belong to Allah. Truly, We directed the People of the Book before you, and you (O Muslims) have reverence for Allah. But (even) if you deny Him, lo! (you should know that) Allah has possession of all things in the heavens and on

*earth; and Allah wants for nothing, and is
worthy of all praise. Yes, to Allah belongs
everything in the heavens and on earth, and
Allah has the power to carry through everything
that happens. If it were His will, He could
destroy you, O humanity, and create another
race; for He has the power to do this.'
(Surah 4:131-133; See also Surahs 5:20; 5:123)*

This, of course, leads us into the perennial logistical
problem of whether it is possible for God to predestine
everything, and yet at the same time grant freewill
to conscious beings. We will look into this problem
in more detail in a later chapter. Suffice it to say
here that if we have no freewill, then we are in no
sense responsible for any of the evil, and may
simply wonder why it is that God has created so
many unpleasant circumstances for us.

3.   GOD EXISTS, BUT IS NOT SUPREME GOOD

Maybe we are misled in thinking that God is a
force for Good. Perhaps that is just wishful thinking,
and He is not benign at all, and actually enjoys
watching victims suffer, and all their hopes getting
cruelly washed away. The peoples of the ancient
world certainly believed that there were 'gods' who
were wilful and capricious, who had to be propitiated
by sacrifices - and even then, there were no guarantees

that one would be safe from such a god's spiteful malevolence.

The Qur'an states that this is a nonsense. Allah cares very much about the fate of His servants:

'Your Lord is Self-sufficient and full of mercy; if it were His will He could destroy you and appoint anyone He chose as your successors, just as He raised you up from the posterity of other people (before you).'   *(Surah 6:133)*

'Glory in the grace and bounty from God, and in the fact that Allah does not suffer the reward of the faithful to be lost (in the least degree). (Surah 5:171)

Allah never enjoys watching people suffer. The Qur'an states:

'Don't lose heart or fall into despair; you must gain mastery if you are true in faith.'   *(Surah 3:139)*

'Truly, your Lord is full of grace towards humanity; even though most of them are ungrateful.'   *(Surah 27:73)*

4. GOD IS AN IMPERSONAL FORCE

It may be that there is a Supreme God, but that we are quite wrong in thinking we are special to Him. Maybe God, in His role as Supreme Power and Originator of the laws of the universe, is just as impersonal as those laws. They operate automatically without any feeling. A falling rock would fall on and crush to death a saint just the same as a sinner. It has nothing to do with the character of the 'victim'. It is quite pointless to appeal to the law of gravity to be merciful. The law is quite inexorable and cannot be appealed to, or special circumstances pleaded. Perhaps the Founder of all laws is the same - a Force rather than a person.

Maybe our belief that He cares about human beings and looks after us in a special way is nothing but wishful thinking on our part. There are millions of life-forms created by our Lord. What gives us the right to assume that we are in any way special to Him? We are less than specks of dust in the universe.

The revealed books, on the contrary, insist that this attitude is quite wrong. God is intimately concerned with very detail of His servants' lives, and knows each one of us personally:

'On Him you should call, and if it be His will, He will remove the distress which was the cause of your call to Him.'   *(Surah 6:41)*

'And We sent messengers only to give good news and to warn; so those who believe and mend (their lives) - upon them shall be no fear nor shall they grieve.'   *(Surah 6:48)*

*'It is He who brought you out from the wombs
of your mothers when you knew nothing; and
He gave you hearing and sight and intelligence
and affection, that you might given thanks
(unto Him).'* (Surah 16:78)

Indeed, Allah is so close to each of us, so intimately
bound up with us, that He knows not only our most
secret thoughts, but even our subconscious thoughts
and emotions that are hidden from our conscious
awareness:

*'It was We who created humanity, and We
know what hidden suggestions each soul makes
to each person; for We are nearer to each
than their jugular vein.'* (Surah 50:16)

5. GOD EXISTS, BUT IS NOT THE CREATOR OF THE UNIVERSE

One way of tackling the problem is to consider
the whole relationship of God to the universe, and
one of the oldest answers to the business of evil was
the suggestion that although there is indeed a Supreme
God who exists over all, He belongs to a realm of
pure spirit, and has nothing whatsoever to do with
the physical universe. The Being we think of as our
God was not really the Creator at all.

The realm of matter must, therefore, have been
the creation of a lesser and inferior semi-god whose

object was actually malign - it was to trap free
spirits into the world of matter, where they certainly
would suffer. This was the theory favoured by
Gnosticism. The aim of humanity in a Gnostic
system was a search for enlightenment, and the
finding of a Saviour who would enable all the
trapped souls or spirits to escape back to their
proper abode in the spiritual 'realm of light'.

The Qur'an casts aside this suggestion. Allah
alone was responsible for creation, and is in command
of all knowledge about it:

> *'With Him are the keys of the Unseen, the
> treasures that none knows but He. He knows
> whatever is in the earth and in the sea. Not a
> leaf falls but with His knowledge. There is not
> a grain in the darkness of the earth, not anything
> green or withered, but it is written in a record
> clear to those who can read it.'*
>
> *(Surah 6:59)*

> *'Say: Do you see what it is you invoke besides
> God? Show me what it is they have created on
> earth, or have they a share in the heavens?
> Bring me a book revealed before this, or any
> remnant of knowledge, if you are telling the
> truth.'*   *(Surah 46:4)*

> *'We created the heavens and the earth and all*

*between them in six days[1], nor did any sense of
weariness touch us.'*   *(Surah 50:38)*

*'With power and skill did We construct the
firmament; for it is We who create the vastness
of space.'*   *(Surah 51:47)*

6.   PANTHEISM - EVERYTHING IS PART OF A WHOLE

Instead of an inferior Creator-God, the Hindu and
Buddhist faiths regard the physical universe with all
its problems as part of a 'telescoping' system which
will eventually 'fold back' into its original Oneness.
Their 'escape system' from the evils of the material
world is through the process of reincarnation (earthly
rebirths, as many times as it takes to reach
enlightenment).

Reincarnation teaches that people are reborn on
earth in a more or less fortunate set of circumstances
and awareness according to their karma (deserved
fate). Souls would either sink further into the depths
of matter, or lift themselves out of it, according to
their deserved fates, inexorably based on the actions
of their lives.

---

1.   A 'day' in creation, before the creation of the sun and moon
anyway, is not to be thought of as our 'familiar' 24-hour day.
It is a period of unknown length, and could represent a period
of thousands or millions of years. See Surah 22:47; 32:5;
70:4.

There are two kinds of reincarnation systems – one that takes beings up and down through the range of all creation, from inanimate objects to animate, and then through plants and animal forms to human and enlightened human; and one that takes human beings up or down from a very basic level of humanity to that of spiritual awareness, then release.

In systems such as these, evil is regarded as part and parcel of physical existence, and the whole object of life becomes an attempt to raise the soul out of physical existence altogether.

In the end, human souls will be absorbed back into the Godhead; the whole system is One.

The Qur'an is adamant that this is a complete fallacy. No human soul can ever 'become' God, or has ever been part of God:

> *'They (i.e. unbelievers) attribute to some of His servants a share with Him (in His Godhead)! These humans are surely blasphemous and ungrateful!'*   *(Surah 43:15)*

> *'Those whom they invoke besides God have no power of intercession; only he who bears witness to the Truth, and they know (him). If you ask them who created them, they will certainly say: God.'*   *(Surah 43:86-87)*

Even that most perfect of human messengers, the Blessed Jesus (ﷺ), stressed that he was:

'No more than a servant. We granted our favour to him, and We made him an example to the children of Israel. And if it were Our will, We could make angels from amongst you, succeeding each other on the earth.' *(Surah 43:59-60)*

Moreover, Jesus (ﷺ) said clearly :

'Now I have come to you with wisdom, and in order to make clear to you some of the points on which you dispute; therefore, fear God and obey me. As for God, He is my Lord and your Lord; so worship Him. This is the straight way.' *(Surah 43:63-64)*

The Qur'an insists that Allah is not in any way a part of His own Creation; as Creator, He is outside anything that was created, and totally Other in nature:

'He is the Irresistible, (watching) from above over His worshippers; and He is the Wise, knowing all things.' *(Surah 6:18)*

'He is the Irresistible (watching) from above over His worshippers; and He sets guardians over you. In due course, when death approaches any of you, Our angels take his soul, and they never fail in their duty.' *(Surah 6:61)*

'Glory to the Lord of the heavens and the earth, the Lord of the Throne! He is (free) from the things they attribute to Him.'

(Surah 43:82)

There is no possibility mentioned in the Qur'an of reincarnation. Allah outlines quite a different fate for humanity after their earthly lives. What will happen to people will depend very much on two things - their beliefs, and how they have lived:

'In the end will they return to their Lord, and We shall then reveal to them the truth of all that they did.' *(Surah 6:108)*

'Allah is the Protector of those who have faith; from the depths of darkness He will lead them forth into light. Of those who reject faith, the patrons are the evil ones; from light they will lead them forth into the depths of darkness. They will be companions of the Fire, to dwell therein (forever). *(Surah 2:257)*

'On that day when every soul will be confronted with all the good it has done and all the evil it has done, it will wish there were a great distance between it and its evil.'(Surah 3:30)

'Do not think of those who are slain in Allah's service as being dead. No, they live, finding their sustenance in the Presence of their Lord.'

(Surah 3:169)

7. DUALISM – THAT GOD HAS AN EQUAL ENEMY, THE POWER OF EVIL.

Some people suggest that God is opposed all the time by another Super-Power, the force of Evil or Darkness. They think that these two exist like the two sides of a coin, and that one is meaningless without the other. Just as one cannot conceive of light without darkness, or the inside of a thing without an outside, so if there is no such thing as Evil then one cannot really talk of Goodness. A thing is only good if there is something less-good with which to compare it. It seems that the two concepts are necessary to each other, like the positive and negative forces in the world of 'matter'.

Whereas there is obvious truth in the philosophy that one could not even begin to recognise Good without Evil with which to compare it, the Qur'an makes it quite specific that the Devil is not equal to God, and never has been:

'Not equal are things that are bad and things that are good, even though the abundance of the bad may dazzle you. Fear God, O ye that understand, that you may prosper.'

(Surah 5:103)

'Repel evil with that which is best.'

(Surah 23:96)

'Satan makes people promises and creates in

them false desires; but Satan's promises are nothing but deception.'   *(Surah 4:120)*

'Yet they make the jinns equal with God, though God created the jinns; and they falsely, having no knowledge, attribute to Him sons and daughters. Praise and glory be to Him! For He is above what they attribute to Him!
                                        (Surah 6:100)

'Do those who practise evil think that they will get the better of us? Evil is their judgement!'
                                        (Surah 29:4)

'Not equal are the blind and those who see; nor are equal those who believe and work deeds of righteousness and those who do evil.'
                                        (Surah 40:58)

Dualists argue that there can never be a final harmony, but that Good and Evil are utterly opposed to each other for all time; the duality can only be overcome by one destroying the other, but that would overthrow the very balance that allows the world to exist.

The Qur'an, on the contrary, maintains that the conflict between God and Satan and its results for humanity will certainly not last for ever:

'We shall expel out of you all the evil in you, and admit you to a gate of great honour.'
                                        (Surah 4:31)

'Those who believe fight in the cause of God,
and those who reject faith fight in the cause of
Evil. So you fight against the friends of Satan!
Feeble indeed is the cunning of Satan.'

(Surah 4:76)

'Do they not know that for those who oppose
God and His Messengers is the Fire of Hell,
wherein they shall dwell? That is the supreme
disgrace.' *(Surah 9:63)*

Christians also accept the notion of an evil force
opposing God, but that God is by definition Supreme;
and, therefore, Christians insist that whatever the
situation now, God will triumph in the end, and the
Devil, whatever he or it may be, will be subjected
to God's power. Naturally, there is no way of
proving this, and it does not explain the reason for
the existence of the Devil in the first place! Why, if
God created the universe, did He create the possibility
of evil at all?

Muslims, and all those who believe in the One
True God, maintain that there is always a way to
defeat evil, and that is to overcome it with good:

'Those who patiently persevere, seeking the
countenance of their Lord, establish regular
prayers, spend out of the gifts We have bestowed
for their sustenance, secretly and openly, these

turn off evil with good; for such there is the
final attainment of the Eternal Home.'
(Surah 13:22)

'Truth stands out clear from error. Whoever
rejects evil and believes in God has grasped
the most trustworthy hand-hold that never
breaks.'   *(Surah 2:256)*

'God will cancel anything that Satan throws
in; and God will confirm His signs.'
(Surah 22:52)

8.   THE DEVIL IS PART OF GOD

Some people believe that since God includes
everything that exists within Himself in some way,
then we should also be bound to accept that the
Devil is also part of God.

This is shown in the Qur'an to be a nonsense; the
Devil is God's sworn enemy, and not in any way a
'part' of Him:

*'God has full knowledge of your enemies; God
is enough for your Protector, and God is enough
as your Helper.'*   *(Surah 4:45)*

*'Whoever is an enemy to God and His angels
and messengers Lo! God is an enemy to those
rejecters of faith.'*   *(Surah 2:98)*

*'O you who believe! Enter into Islam
wholeheartedly, and follow not the footsteps of*

the Evil One; for he is to you an avowed enemy.' *(Surah 2:208; also 6:142).*

God is the sole source of all that is created, whether visible in this world or invisible. A lovely passage in the Old Testament, revealed by Allah to the Prophet Isaiah (ﷺ) reads : 'I am the Lord, there is no other; I make the light, I create darkness, author alike of prosperity and trouble. I, the Lord, do all these things.' *(Isaiah 45:6-7)*

God is beyond all description, even the categories of good and evil. The Devil is in no way part of God - but in His creative acts God has laid His creatures open both to beneficial forces that promote health and happiness, and also destructive forces whose end is suffering and annihilation. Which of these is activated depends on the free choice of each creative.

9. THE CONCEPT OF 'EVIL' IS SUBJECTIVE, AND THEREFORE, A MEANINGLESS ILLUSION

A different kind of theory maintains that we are wrong in labelling certain things as 'evil' - this is a subjective and meaningless delusion. If we could just stand right back and see the universe as a whole, we would be able to understand that it does form one ultimate unit, and that every part of it follows natural laws which cannot really be labelled as either good or evil. We would be obliged to look at things from a much higher point of view, and not just our rather selfish human angle.

Just thinking about our planet alone, other living organisms must surely have as much right to their life and destiny as human beings, and since all the species depend for their lives on eating each other in some way, individual tragedies can only really be considered as a part of the total pattern.

Put a human down in the jungle, and he will soon become part of a lion or a hyaena or a vulture; put him down amongst civilisation, and he still does not escape - he will be eaten by germs. This may be unfortunate for him, but it is not 'evil' - simply part of the way things are in Nature. The microbe that inflicts fatal disease does not regard itself as evil - it is simply living its own life-cycle. Perhaps if we could see the whole as God sees it, we would regard the natural cycle of living matter through various bodies as being perfectly in order, and not complain about it.

The Qur'an recognises human blindness in recognising the importance and significance of other 'communities' of life, and their rights, and gives lessons:

*'There is not an animal (that lives) on the
earth, not a being that flies on its wings, but
forms communities like you. Nothing have We
omitted from the Book, and they all shall be
gathered to their Lord in the end.'*

(Surah 6:38)

'My mercy extends to all things.'

(Surah 7:156)

*'At length, when they came to a valley of ants,
one of the ants said : O ye ants, get into your
habitations, lest Solomon and his hosts crush
you (under foot) without knowing it!'*

(Surah 27:18)

Abd Allah b. Masud reported : 'We were with the
Apostle of Allah (ﷺ) during a journey. We saw a
bird with her two young ones and we captured the
young. The bird came and began to spread its
wings. The Apostle of Allah (ﷺ) came and said:
'Who made this suffer for its young ones? Return
the young ones to it.'

He also saw an ant colony that we had burnt. He
asked: 'Who has burnt this?' We replied: 'We did.'
He said: 'It is not proper to punish with fire except
the Lord of Fire.'   (Abu Dawud 2669).

However, to state that evil does not really exist
and is just an illusion does not prevent us from
finding pain and cruelty in our world. These are our

data, and it is no more than evading the issue to postulate an eternal standpoint from which we can wish them away. Animals use other animals unmercifully for their own ends, none more cruelly and wantonly than Man, armed as he is with immense intelligence and cunning. In any case, if we are only imagining that we are suffering that is no help whatsoever - imagining that we are suffering is bad enough, and to be told that we are mistaken in this imagination only makes us feel worse!

10. EVIL IS JUST A 'NEGATIVE'

Just as blindness is the absence of sight, and darkness is the absence of light, so perhaps evil is eventually just the absence of good and is only a 'negative' with no substantive existence of its own. This is not a satisfactory answer, for we are hardly correct in believing that blindness and darkness are no more than 'absences' of something. Maybe it is the other way round, and light is simply the absence of darkness?

To define evil merely as a deficiency of goodness rather than the presence of bad ignores the fact that our actual feelings and states of affairs have very real and painful existences. The barbarity of humans to their fellows, their unsurpassed cruelty to each other, suggests there is far more to evil than mere absence of goodness.

11. EVIL IS USEFUL

Some people try to diminish suffering and evil by pointing out their usefulness. Pain tells you when something is going wrong with your body. Burning teaches you not to play with fire, and can be tamed and used to cook things, drive engines, warm homes, and so on. This is an important point and we will look into this in more detail later. However, not all pain is useful, or produces a greater good. So although the theory apparently 'reduces' the problem, it certainly does not answer it.

12. SPINOZA'S THEORY OF NECESSARY EVIL AS PART OF THE 'COMPLETE' UNIVERSE

The Jewish philosopher Spinoza worked out this idea to its full conclusions. If the complete reality was just one perfect 'system', in which every single thing followed its course by logical necessity, then obviously nothing existed by accident, but everything was determined by law according to the will of God. The only exception was God Himself, Who alone was not determined by anything outside Himself.

Allah reveals in the Holy Qur'an that it is certainly true that nothing happens by accident :

'Say: Who then has the least power against God, if His will were to destroy Christ the son

> *of Mary, his mother, and all - every one that*
> *is on the earth? For to God belong the dominion*
> *of the heavens and the earth, and all that is*
> *between. He creates what He pleases. For God*
> *has power over all things.'*   *(Surah 5:19)*

> *'If God touches you with affliction, none can*
> *remove it but He; if He touch you with happiness,*
> *He has power over all things.'   (Surah 6:17)*

Spinoza then went on to argue that it was logically impossible that things could be any better than they were, since everything that happened was due to the activity of God. Therefore, everything that seemed to be bad or evil was just due to our lack of awareness and understanding, the fact that our minds and our knowledge are limited, and that it is not possible for us to understand the infinite perfection of the system. Good and evil, then, do not exist as such, but are ideas in our minds formed by our habits or comparing the goodness or usefulness of things for ourselves.

The limitations of our knowledge are stressed in the Qur'an for it is a human weakness to wish to know the reason why everything is as it is, and why people should have to suffer. The Muslim is expected to accept whatever God sends with patience and endurance, and not to waste time seeking to understand the reasons why, which are beyond us:

'That is God your Lord! There is no God but He, the Creator of all things; then worship Him; He has the power to dispose all affairs. No vision can grasp Him, but His grasp is over all vision; He is above all comprehension, yet Himself knows all things.'

(Surah 6:102-103)

None in the heavens or on earth, except God, knows what is hidden; nor can they perceive when they shall be raised up for judgement. Still less can their knowledge comprehend the Hereafter; no, they are in doubt and uncertainty.'

(Surah 27:65-66)

'Truly the knowledge of the Hour is with God alone; it is He who sends down rain, and He Who knows what is in the wombs. Nor does anyone know what it is that he will earn tomorrow; nor does anyone know in what land he will die. Truly full knowledge is with God, and He knows all things.'   *(Surah 31:34)*

Abu Hurayrah reported : 'Allah's Apostle (ﷺ) said that Allah the Exalted, the Glorious, said : 'I have prepared for my pious servants that which no eye has ever seen, and no ear has ever heard, and no human heart has ever perceived it, but it is testified by the Book of Allah.' He then recited: *'No soul knows what comfort has been concealed from them,*

*as a reward for what they did.' (Surah 32:17)
(Hadith Muslim 6780)*

Once people have persuaded themselves that
everything exists for their sake, then they naturally
see things as being evil or unfortunate to them.
Spinoza thought that we were quite wrong to imagine
that everything was made for our benefit. He argued
that a complete or perfect universe would have in it
the full range of experiences and beings - the lower
as well as the higher. A universe which had only the
higher kind of being (whatever that might be!)
would not logically be as perfect as one containing
the whole range. Therefore, to express the infinite
creative activity of God, the sinner must exist as
well as the saint.

13. GOD'S JUSTICE WORKS OUT IN ANOTHER WORLD

Going off on a different tack, some people think
that perhaps God does exist and does care, but He
makes up to us in another world for what we suffer
in this one. Our reward will depend quite a lot on
how we tackled the tests and trials of this life. A
life after death then becomes a necessity, if God is
to work out justice for us all. We get our 'pie in the
sky'.

The Qur'an reveals that this argument is well on
the right lines, for very different fates await those

who have striven to do God's will and have lived
decent and honest lives from those who have been
selfish and greedy and oppressive:

'On that Day the dominion will be that of God;
He will judge between them; so those who
believe and work righteous deeds will be in
gardens of delight, and for those who reject
faith and deny Our signs there will be a
humiliating punishment.'   *(Surah 22:56-57)*

'If any do good, good will accrue to them from
it, and they will be secure from terror that
Day. And if any do evil, their faces will be
thrown headlong into the Fire. 'Do you receive
a reward other than that which you earned by
your deeds?'   *(Surah 27:89-90)*

'He that works evil will not be requited but by
the like thereof; and he that works a righteous
deed - whether man or woman - and is a
believer - such will enter the Garden of Bliss.'
(Surah 40:40)

'What? Do those who seek after evil ways
think that We shall hold them equal with those
who believe and do righteous deeds - that
equal will be their life and their death? Ill is
the judgement that they make.'
(Surah 45:21)

*'Yes, to God belongs all that is in the heavens
and on earth; so that He rewards those who do
evil according to their deeds, and he rewards
those who do good with what is best.'*[2]

(Surah 53:31)

However, the idea still haunts us that there could
have been a different way of arranging things, that
surely it was unnecessary to evolve rational beings
out of a material world with all the attendant sorrows
of the process.

If people (or their souls?) can live in heaven,
why bother with earth and all its struggles, and
hardships? If rational beings can have existence
beyond the realm of space and time, why was it
necessary to plunge them into a spatio-temporal
cosmos?

Those who believe in heaven are always tempted
to use this belief to justify the problems and sufferings
of this world - no doubt we can enjoy the hope that
the glories of heaven will far outweigh the most
excruciating of sufferings. However, the very
possibility of such a beatific existence leads us to

---

2.   This is a lovely evidence of Allah's justice tempered with
     mercy. Our punishment for the evil we have done is fair and
     balanced; but our reward for the good we have done is
     magnified out of all proportion by Allah's kindness and
     generosity, and love for us.

wonder why God was not content just to have made us for that world in the first place, and not ploughed us into the maelstrom of this life.

14. THERE HAS NOT BEEN A 'FALL', AND THERE IS NO INHERITED SIN

Evolutionists do not accept the notion of the Fall of Man from a state of goodness and bliss. They see, rather, the gradual progress towards morality from an original state of ignorance and savagery - not so much a 'fall' of Man as a 'rise'. Perhaps the whole universe is evolving towards a state of deeper awareness or consciousness, which brings with it a greater freedom of the will and also a greater burden of responsibility.

Teilhard de Chardin, a Jesuit priest and archaeologist, followed up this train of thought. He suggested that we had travelled from primitive and brutish ancestors along a line of progress towards perfection, an evolution of morality and goodness. He thought that as Humanity became more conscious of itself as 'beings', they would gradually become aware of the concept of Humanity as a whole, of the entire human race as being 'brothers', one ummah.

So humans would come to care more for the needs and happiness of others, and at the same time consciousness would become more and more acute until humanity reached the stage of awareness of God, and mystical union with God. At this stage, the human race would have reached maturity. However, in order for this to happen, suffering and pain and moral evil had to exist as part of that process of growth.

Spiritual evolution can only take place if there is free will, and for free will to exist, there has to be the possibility of making wrong or immoral choices, or of doing some things that are less good than others. This must mean that in order to be free we are bound to live in an environment full of dangers and challenges, an environment in which the results of our own free choices can damage others.

What is morally intolerable in this argument is that in order to produce the end-product of enlightened conscious beings, untold millions of animals and species have had to fight and die and suffer on behalf of an end-product they could not conceivably value. Does this not seem worse than the cruelties of those regimes - to sacrifice the comfort and happiness of one group or even an entire generation in order to produce benefits for the next? If turns the notion of evolution into a ghastly charade of progress.

We cannot get out of it by supposing that lesser life forms do not feel pain. They may not suffer as intensely as we think, or they may suffer in a totally different way. Nor can Muslims take refuge in the Hindu doctrine of reincarnation and Karma - that the suffering of an animal (or human) is the consequence of sin in an earlier life, and gives the creature the change of a higher form of life in some future birth.

To put it simply, if we saw a wounded creature or human by the roadside, we could not just pass by on the other side, and still regard ourselves as good Muslims.

These are all clever theories, put forward by clever minds. Even so, there remains a gut feeling that the presence of such things as hatred, envy, malice, fear, despair, contempt, pride, shame, cruelty, cowardice, avarice and lust still need an explanation, if we are to accept that God is Creator and His creation is good.

CHAPTER THREE

AN ANSWER TO THE PROBLEM OF EVIL SUGGESTED IN THE OLD TESTAMENT

Biblical opinions about suffering depend on which Testament you are reading. In the Old Testament, one of the most interesting theological works is the book of Job, the story of a legendary and long suffering sheikh of the 'land of Uz', who may possibly have been a citizen of Petra in North West Arabia at the time when it was a 'city of tents'. He was presumably a member of either the 'Ad or Thamud tribes (cf Surahs 7:65-72 etc). This book should be of great interest to Muslims, for it is the only 'Muslim' book in the Bible, and the devout sheikh Job is better known to Muslims as Nabi Ayyub (ﷺ).

The whole theme of his story in the Bible is the problem of evil and suffering. Most religious people at that time believed that people would be fortunate and healthy if they lived good lives, but if they did evil then God would punish them with sickness and misfortune. No one could deceive God - He would know who was good and who was evil, and His justice would be fair and beyond reproach. But would it?

Job's experience is presented in the Old Testament as that of a good man who suffered terribly, and could think of nothing that he had done to deserve it, simply because Satan saw how devout he was and requested God for permission to test him (Cf Job 1:6-12). His friends believed his troubles had beset him because he lacked faith in God. He should have been repenting and praying for healing. Their belief came with the usual conclusion that failure to be healed is a proof that one's 'faith' is not strong enough. This very common belief - which masquerades as piety and submission to God - is in fact very misguided. Although well-meant, it really is a cruel attitude which condemns any poor invalid to mental torment and guilt on top of his or her physical sufferings!

At first, Job commanded enormous respect as an eminent elder. 'When I went out to the gate of the city... the young men saw me and withdrew, the aged rose up and stood; princes refrained from talking.' .... 'I was a father to the poor, and I searched out the cause of him I did not know. I broke the fangs of the unrighteous, and made him drop his prey from his teeth.' (Job 29:7-10, 16-17)

Unfortunately, when they saw disasters strike him, the attitude of the people changed. They made sport of him, the lowest of the low were able to sneer at him. Job was afflicted by terrible sickness, his children died, he lost all his wealth and possessions, and was rejected by his wife. This wife suggested that he 'curse God and die!' - but Job was the model of Islamic patience, and took the attitude : 'Shall we receive good at the hand of God and not accept the evil?'   (Job 2:10)

Job did not agree at all with the limited interpretation of the masses. He tried to show, in a most moving way, that his sufferings were not damning evidence of Divine judgement on him (as his friends piously sought to establish), but were actually a proof of Divine confidence in him.

His story as presented in the Old Testament in fact gives a striking reminder of the inadequacy of human horizons for any proper understanding of the problem of suffering except that counselled by Islam. Since no human beings are in a position to know God's will, except to be sure that what God plans and intends *will* come to pass, it is their duty to submit and accept.

This was stated by Job's 'comforter' Elihu in chapter 35 - 'If you do evil, you only harm yourself and not God. What are your sins to Him? Similarly, if you do good, you do not give anything to Him, and He does not receive from your hand. The good and evil that you do concerns only yourself.'

As the Qur'an states:

'O humanity! It is you that have need of God; but God is the One free of all wants, worthy of all praise.'   (Surah 35:15; see also 31:26).

'Those who reject God (and) hinder (people) from the path of God, and resist the Messenger after guidance has been clearly shown to them, will not injure God in the least.'

(Surah 47:32)

The saint is the person who can accept whatever life places in front of him or her without complaint against God or losing faith in God - the position finally arrived at by Job after he worked through a time of great depression. In the midst of his suffering, he remained submitted to God. He 'held tight to the Rope', and nothing shook his faith in the existence of God, or God's justice, or that God would eventually vindicate him.

'I know that my Vindicator lives.... and after my skin has been destroyed, then outside my flesh I shall see God. I shall see for myself, my eyes shall behold, and not another's.'   (Job 19:25-26).

The book ends with a splendid vision of God, in which Job's understanding is not much deeper than before, but his faith in God is affirmed and he is comforted and restored.

It is so moving a text that many Christians have wished to see in it a form of Christianity before Christ - but in this they are searching a blind alley. There is no place in Job's theology for a saviour, a dying and rising god-man taking on himself the sins of the world and transmuting them. Job considered that kind of thinking to be the very temptation offered by the Triad or Trinitarian cults,[3] including the Al-Uzzah and Manat cults of Petra. In the Book of Job what we really have is precisely what the Muslims claim about the Prophet Ayyub - that he was a Muslim before the revelation of the Qur'an.

Basically, his book (as it stands in the Old Testament) concluded that the realm of God is far beyond the power of human understanding, but that

---

3.   It was commonplace throughout the ancient world to think of God with a family – Father, Mother and a Divine Som who usually had to die as a sacrifice and be restored to life in order to procure the salvation of those who believed. Interested readers could refer to my books 'Have the Christians got it All Wrong?', Muslim Academic Trust, 1999; and 'What Every Christian Need to Know about Islam', Islamic Foundation, Markfield Dawah Dentre, Leicestershire, UK, 1999.

once people catch a brief glimpse of all that God's work involves, they submit. They cease to complain but stand trembling and silent before His incomprehensible Majesty and Sovereignty.

Allah counsels acceptance in the pages of the Qur'an. Suffering is the greatest bestower of experience, out of which comes growth. Muslims are requested to face suffering with patience and endurance, and try to see in the midst of their sufferings what it is that God requires them to do, and how He requires them to behave:

'And We shall try you until We test those among you who strive their utmost and persevere in patience; and We shall try your reported mettle.' (Surah 47:31)

'Be not weary and faint-hearted, crying for peace, when you should be uppermost; for Allah is with you, and will never put you in loss for your good deeds.' (Surah 47:35)

'Muhammad is the Messenger of God; and those who are with him are strong against unbelievers, but compassionate amongst each other. You will see them bow and prostrate themselves, seeking grace from God and His good pleasure. On their faces are their marks,

*the traces of their prostration. This is their
similitude in the Taurat. And their similitude
in the Gospel is like a seed which sends forth
its blade, then makes it strong; it then becomes
thick, and it stands on its own stem, filling the
sowers with wonder and delight.'*

(Surah 48:29)

*'Man can have nothing but what he strives for;
and the fruit of his striving will soon come in
sight.'*   *(Surah 53:39-40)*

*'It is He who sends down tranquillity into the
hearts of believers, that they may add faith to
their faith.'*   *(Surah 48:4)*

*'For in God's sight are all His servants....
Those who show patience, firmness and self-
control; who are true, who worship devoutly,
who spend in the way of God, and who pray
for forgiveness in the early hours of the
morning.'*   *(Surah 3:15-17)*

*'How many of the Prophets fought, and with
them large bands of godly men? But they never
lost heart. If they met with disaster in God's
service, neither did they weaken nor give in.
God loves those who are firm and steadfast.'*

(Surah 3:146)

This must have been particularly true of the long-suffering Ayyub (ﷺ)!

His story reveals the reward that comes eventually to those who hold fast.

> *'Obey God and His messenger, and fall into no disputes, lest you lose heart and your power depart; be patient and persevering, for God is with those who patiently persevere.'*
>
> *(Surah 8:46)*

> *'We shall certainly bear with patience all the hurt you may cause us; for those who put their trust should put their trust in Allah.'*
>
> *(Surah 14:12)*

> *'But if any show patience and forgive, that would truly be an exercise of courageous will and resolution in the conduct of affairs.'*
>
> *(Surah 42:43)*

As it is summed up by the beautiful Surah 'Asr:

> *'By (the token of) Time (through the Ages), truly humanity is in loss except such as have faith, and do righteous deeds, and (join together) in the mutual teaching of truth, and of patience and constancy.'* *(Surah 103)*

CHAPTER FOUR

ONE ANSWER TO THE PROBLEM OF EVIL SUGGESTED IN THE NEW TESTAMENT

In the New Testament - all the books of which are about Jesus (ﷺ), and the first of which was written some thirty years after his death - the Blessed Jesus (ﷺ) is portrayed not only as Messiah of Israel but also as a great teacher and healer. His many miracles of healing show very clearly that the idea of God being cruel and vindictive, striking people down with sickness and suffering, is not true. The teachings are an excellent antidote to those pious well-meaning folk who comment helplessly that the diseases have to be accepted and put up with, as they are 'God's will'. The activity of Jesus (ﷺ), as portrayed in the Gospels, shows that sufferings are never the will of God, but of God's enemy.

The reaction of Jesus (ﷺ) when confronted with sickness was always to heal, to put right again. He could cure the complete personality, physical, mental and spiritual. Healings are recorded of physical disorders (such as poorly arms, legs, eyes and skin, and virus and bone infections), mental disorders (such as epilepsy and paralysis), and spiritual disorders caused by demon possession.

Sometimes he healed by prayer alone, and sometimes by mechanical means, using touch and saliva (Mark 7:31-37, 8:22-26; John 9). Sometimes he laid his hand on the affected part of the person (Mark 1:29-31, 1:40-45, 5:21-43, 9:14-29; Luke 13:10-17, 14:1-6, 22:47-51; John 18:10-11). Sometimes he healed from a distance by commanding the sickness to leave the person (cf Mark 1:21-28, 3:1-6, 5:1-20), sometimes he helped people to see that their sins were forgiven, and relieved sufferings caused by guilt (Mark 2:1-13; John 5:1-14), and sometimes he recognised that their suffering was indeed caused by an evil spirit, that had to be removed (Mark 1:21-28, 5:1-20; 9:14-29).

Sometimes the cure came about helped by the faith of the invalid (Mark 10:46-52; Luke 17:11-19) and sometimes by the faith of another person who cared about the invalid (Mark 7:24-30; Luke 7:1-10; 7:11-17; Matthew 8:5-13, 15:21-28; John 2:46-54). Sometimes their faith did not come into it at all - they were unaware of the healing attempt, they were unconscious, or they were even dead!

Jesus' healings were famous successes. During his three year ministry he was followed by large crowds of invalids wherever he went. Sometimes, we are told, he did not even take the time off to eat. (Mark 6:30)

He would probably have had very little patience with the reaction of someone at a child's sickbed who declared that it must be God's will that the child was in distress. However, it was vitally important to Jesus that people should not simply go to him to receive bodily health. He had a lot more to offer, a far richer reward than simply a longer life here - for which the end at some time or other will always be death.

An examination of his healing ministry leads one to several important conclusions. If the narratives are true, and Jesus really did heal sickness, and even raise people from the dead, then the sickness *cannot* have been inflicted as the will of God in the first place, for if it had been the will of God, then nothing Jesus said or did could have made any difference.

As one cured blind man put it: 'We know that God does not listen to sinners, but if anyone is a worshipper of God and does His will, God listens to him. Never since the world began has it been heard that anyone opened the eyes of a man born blind. If this man (Jesus (ﷺ)) were not from God, he could do nothing.' (John 9:31-33)

Secondly, sickness should not be seen as a punishment sent by God for our sins (as it specifically states people believed to be the case in John 9:2 - 'Rabbi, who sinned, this man or his parents, that he was born blind?'), except in so far as we punish ourselves for our wrongdoing by such things as repressing guilt, or damaging our bodies by indulgence in harmful practices like breathing in nicotine and tar or poisoning ourselves with alcohol and drugs.

Although Jesus (ﷺ) often ended the day exhausted, he used prayer and contact with God to renew his strength, rather than simply fall asleep. (see Mark 1:35; Luke 5:16; 6:12; 9:18)

His ministry reveals his great love, compassion and self-denial, for he had not come primarily as a healer, and the work with invalids must often have exhausted him and impeded his progress as a Messenger. Yet he never turned people away. Even a visit from his own family had to take second place to his great work. Nothing distracted him from it. Even in the excitement of his arrest, after his agony of mind in the Garden of Gethsemane, he paused to heal the stricken ear of an enemy. (Luke 22:47-51)

The ability of Jesus (ﷺ) to work miracles of healing does not suggest to a Muslim, however, that this proves he was the 'Son of God'. On the contrary, they point out that the ministry was not confined to Jesus (ﷺ), but he passed on the ability to his disciples, and they could all heal. They were even sent out on practice missions during his lifetime (Luke (9:16). After Jesus' (ﷺ) departure the ability of the disciples to heal was one of the chief marks of their calling, and the gift spread to many of the early Christians. For example, Ananias of Damascus cured Paul's blindness (Acts 9:17-19). The ability to heal was seen not as a challenge to the will of God (which was supposed to have been to punish people by inflicting them with suffering!), but as the direct action of the Spirit of God to heal and make whole. All possessors of the Holy Spirit were healers in one sense or another. The important ingredients were prayer, right living and self-control; believers had to bring themselves into the Presence of God, and become open to His power.

When Muslims counsel patience and steadfastness in the face of suffering, in similar manner it does not mean that they believe God has callously inflicted this suffering just because He felt like it, or as a punishment. Although some suffering certainly falls upon humanity as the inevitable result of their wrongdoings and deviation from the 'Straight Path', the vast majority of our sufferings are inflicted by God's enemy. The sufferings that are a punishment from God are matters of the next life, the Hereafter, and not of this.

It is difficult for non-Muslims to understand how Muslims can accept all eventualities as being the will of God, and yet at the same time continue to fight against evil. The Muslim concepts will be considered in detail in the next chapter.

At this stage, let us simply consider the sunnah, the example of the Blessed Prophet Muhammad (ﷺ), and see how closely it agrees with the mind and philosophy of the Blessed Jesus (ﷺ).

For a start - and it is a very important start - all Muslims are aware that even the very best of Muslims sometimes go through appalling suffering. They suffer just as much as non-Muslims from stupendous natural disasters, from diseases, from warfare, persecution, and so on. So did the Blessed Prophet (ﷺ) himself - he suffered wounds, deprivation, torment, abuse, hardship, drought, poisoning, and much more - and ultimately, death.

Secondly, according to Abu Musa al-Ashari, the Prophet (ﷺ) left very clear instructions that his followers were to work for healing and the relieving of suffering, and not just sit back and do nothing about them:

'Feed the hungry, visit the sick and free the captive.'   *(Hadith Abu Dawud 3099)*

The Prophet himself (ﷺ) made a practise of visiting the sick regularly, and praying for them.

The daughter of Sa'd b. Abu Waqqas recorded that her father said: 'I had a complaint at Makkah. The Apostle of Allah (ﷺ) came to pay a sick-visit to me. He put his hand on my forehead, stroked my chest and belly, and then said : *'O Allah! heal up Sa'd and complete his immigration.'*
(Abu Dawud 3098)

Zayd b.Arqam said: *'The Apostle of Allah (ﷺ) visited me while I was suffering from pain in my eyes.'*   *(Abu Dawud 3096)*

Aishah recorded that when Sa'd b. Muadh suffered on the Day of the Trench when a man shot an arrow in the vein of his band, the Apostle of Allah (ﷺ) pitched a tent for him in the mosque so that he might visit him from near at hand.'
(Abu Dawud 3095)

In fact, Anas b. Malik recorded the Blessed Prophet (ﷺ) as saying:

'If anyone performs ablution well and pays a sick-visit to his brother Muslim seeking his reward from Allah, he will be removed a distance of sixty years from Hell.'   *(Abu Dawud 3091)*

The Prophet (ﷺ) taught that Allah acknowledged people's sufferings, and that their sufferings could even be a means of purifying them from their sins:

Umm al-Ala reported: The Apostle of Allah (ﷺ) visited me while I was sick. He said: 'Be glad, Umm al-Ala, for Allah removes the sins of a Muslim on account of illness as fire removes the dross of gold and silver.' *(Hadith Abu Dawud 3086)*

The Prophet (ﷺ) did not limit his ministry of healing to those who were already Muslim. He went out to seek and save people of all types and religions, simply on humanitarian grounds. For example:

Anas reported: A young Jew became ill. The Prophet (ﷺ) went to visit him. He sat down by his head and said to him: 'Accept Islam.' He looked at his father who was beside him near his head, and he said; 'Obey Abu al-Qasim.' (another name of Muhammad). So he accepted Islam. *(Hadith Abu Dawud 3089)*

When the Prophet (ﷺ) visited sick people, he certainly used to pray for their healing.

Umm Salamah reported: When one of you is afflicted with a calamity, he should say: 'We belong to Allah, and to Him do we return. *(Surah 2:156)* O Allah, I expect reward from Thee for this affliction: so give me reward for it, and give me the better compensation.' *(Abu Dawud 3113)*

It seems that the Prophet (ﷺ) - although he disapproved the use of magical charms and spells - did not disapprove the kind of method of curing an invalid that was reported of the Blessed Jesus (ﷺ), when he used saliva to cure blindness on one occasion, and to heal a deaf-mute on another.

Kharijah b. al-Salt recorded that he passed a clan of Arabs who brought to his paternal uncle a lunatic in chains. The uncle recited Surah al-Fatihah over him for three days, morning and evening. When he finished, he collected his saliva and then spat it out (and he felt relief) as if he were set free from a bond. He then came to the Prophet (ﷺ) and mentioned it to him. The Apostle of Allah (ﷺ) said: 'Accept it, for by my life, some accept it as a worthless charm, but you have done so far a genuine one.'   *(Abu Dawud 3413)*

Aishah the beloved wife of the Prophet (ﷺ) reported: When any person fell ill with a disease or he had any ailment or he had any injury, the Apostle of Allah (ﷺ) placed his forefinger upon the ground and then lifted it reciting the name of Allah (and said): 'The dust of our ground with the saliva of any one of us would serve as a means whereby our illness would be cured, if Allah wills.' (Hadith Muslim 5444. This hadith was transmitted on the authority of Ibn Abu Shajhah and Zubayr with a slight variation of wording).

Aishah also recorded: When any person amongst us fell ill, Allah's Messenger (ﷺ) used to stroke him with his right hand and then say: 'O Lord of the people, grant him health, heal him, for You are the Great Healer. There is no healer, but with Your healing power a person is healed and illness is removed.' She further added, when talking about the Blessed Prophet's (ﷺ) own death: When Allah's Messenger (ﷺ) fell ill, and his illness took a serious turn, I took hold of his hand so that I should do with it what he used to do with it. But he withdrew his hand from my hand and then said : 'O Allah, pardon me and make me join the companionship on high.' She said: 'I was gazing at him constantly as he passed away.' *(Hadith Muslim 5432).*

Other versions of the Prophet's (ﷺ) beautiful prayer are: 'Lord of the people, remove the disease, cure him, for You are the Great Curer, there is no cure but through Your healing power, which leaves nothing of the disease.' (Hadith Muslim 5434), and 'Lord of the people, remove the trouble for in Your hand is the cure; none is there to relieve him but only You.' *(Hadith Muslim 5437)*

Furthermore, Aishah also recorded that the Prophet (ﷺ) commanded the use of incantation for curing the influence of the 'evil eye' (Hadith Muslim 5445-5447), and Anas b. Malik recorded that he had been granted sanction to use incantation for the sting of the scorpion, curing small pustules and dispelling the influence of the 'evil eye' (Hadith Muslim 5448-5457). The incantation used was Surah al-Fatihah.   *(Hadith Muslim 5458-61)*

Uthman b. Abu al-As reported that the Prophet commanded him to 'Place your hand at the place where you feel pain in your body and say 'Bismillah' (in the name of Allah) three times and seven times 'I seek refuge with Allah and with His Power from the evil that I find that I fear.'   *(Hadith Muslim 5462)*

In fact, the Prophet said : 'There is a remedy for every malady, and when the remedy is applied to the disease it is cured, with the permission of Allah, the Exalted, the Glorious.' *(Hadith Muslim 5466)*

Finally, to return now to the teaching of the New Testament, the parable of Blessed Jesus (ﷺ) concerning the Wheat and the Tares indicated one reason why God did not simply just 'weed out' of our wordly life all that caused suffering amongst us. The parable *(Matthew 13:24-30)* taught that the 'Farmer', God, had an enemy, the Devil, and *he* was responsible for the evil and suffering in the world. God certainly knew it was there, and left it there. But why did He leave it there? Two reasons, it seems. Firstly, to give the evil person the greatest possible opportunity to reform and change, and secondly because to destroy all evil persons would be terribly hurtful and damaging to the good - those who loved them.

CHAPTER FIVE

THE REVELATION OF THE HOLY QUR'AN

'God has the key to all secrets. He knows whatever is on the land and in the sea; no leaf falls without His knowing it; there is not a grain in the darkness of earth, or a green or dry thing, but it is carefully noted.' *(Surah 6:59)*

'If God lay the touch of trouble on you, no-one can deliver you from it save God alone; and if He wills good for you, no-one can prevent His blessings. He confers them on His servants as He chooses.' *(Surah 10:107)*

According to the Qur'an the first humans, Adam and Eve, were a male and female made from a single soul. Their story is inseparable from the story of the origin of evil, as it is in the Bible, but the cause of evil in the universe is presented quite differently from the Biblical version. The possibility of humans choosing to do evil stems from God deliberately creating them with freewill, despite the misgivings of the angels.

The humans 'nafs' or soul - could be influenced towards evil by the 'whisperings' of evil spirits, or jinn.

Evil spirits have no place in the universe of the materialists. Many people feel that modern science has explained away everything supernatural, and are embarrassed by the fact that the Blessed Jesus (ﷺ) appeared to believe in evil spirits - indeed, be spent much of his time talking of them and to them, and releasing tormented humans from their clutches. Therefore, they believe Jesus (ﷺ) must have been wrong (that is, influenced by the 'simple' beliefs of his day), and his 'simplicity' proves that he was not gifted with true 'divine knowledge'. The so-called possessed people must have been suffering from mental disorders - schizophrenia, epilepsy, paranoia and the like.

The Qur'an, however, stands solidly behind the pronouncements and activities of the Blessed Jesus (ﷺ) when it comes to confronting evil spirits. It states as a fact that among the unseen things of the universe are at least two orders of non-physical creatures - not only the angels, (special messengers of God), but also the jinn (creatures of fire).

'Praise be to Allah, Who created out of nothing the heavens and the earth, Who made the angels messengers`with wings, two three our four; He adds to Creation as He pleases.'

(Surah 35:1)

'We created humanity from sounding clay, from mud moulded into shape; and the jinn race We had created before, from the fire of a scorching wind.'   *(Surah 15:26-27; 55:15)*

Jinn are not just imaginary beings, but very real, and of considerable power. It is worth pointing out that both 'species' (angels and jinn) existed long before the creation of the human race at a stage when the universe was perfect and human evil did not exist.

According to the Qur'an, the urge to do evil was not caused by the weakness of humanity, or by their greed or lust, or their disobedient nature. It went back beyond those things; humans were indeed weak, but they were unwittingly being used by Shaytan or Iblis, the Devil.

The Qur'an explains the origin of the Devil's animosity towards humans. It began before humans were created. God intended the first man, Adam, to rule the earth and look after it. He ordered all the angels to respect His decision, but the chief jinn, Iblis (or Shaytan - Satan) refused to do this.

'The Lord said to the angels - 'When I have finished Man and breathed My spirit into him, then bow down in obeisance to him. And all the angels bowed down in obeisance. The exception was Iblis, the Devil.'

(Surah 15:29-31).

There are two suggested reasons for this refusal. The Qur'an reveals that he considered himself to be a superior creature to the human and therefore would not bow down.

'(God said), 'What prevented you from bowing down when I commanded you?' He said, 'I am better than he. You created me from fire and him from clay.' *(Surah 7:12)*

Secondly, some Islamic scholars have suggested that jealousy on his own behalf was not the real reason for his disobedience, but it could have been much more pious. It could have been his over-zealous purity and jealousy for God. He may have thought that he 'knew better' than God, and insisted to Allah that he could bow down to none but Him.

Whatever his reason, even if we can grant Shaytan the best of motives, he questioned God's clear command and disobeyed it, and this was the cause of sin. For this he was punished, and, therefore, became the enemy of all humans. Since that time he has done his best to get revenge by leading people's hearts and minds away from God.

*'Iblis said, 'O my Lord! Because you have put
me in the wrong, I will make wrong seem a
good thing to those on earth, and I will put
them all in the wrong.'   (Surah 15:39)*

In the story of Adam and Eve, the human couple
are created perfect but are given freewill, and they
choose to sin. God created a special tree, told Adam
that if he ate of its fruits he would suffer, and then
given him the choice of whether or not to eat them
and the opportunity to do so.

'(God said): O Adam! You and your wife live in
the garden and enjoy (its good things) as you wish;
but do not approach this tree, or you will run into
harm and transgression.' Then Shaytan began to
whisper suggestions to them, bringing openly before
their minds all their shame that was hidden from
them (before). He said: 'Your Lord only forbade
you this tree, lest you should become angels or such
beings as live for ever.'

And he swore to them both that he was their
sincere adviser. So by deceit he brought about their
fall; when they had tasted of the tree their shame
became manifest to them, and they began to sew
together the leaves of the Garden over their bodies.

*And their Lord called unto them: 'Did I not
forbid you that tree, and tell you that Shaytan
was an avowed enemy to you?' They said:*

*'Our Lord! We have wronged our own souls; if
You do not forgive us and do not bestow Your
mercy upon us, we shall be lost indeed.' God
said: 'Get you down, with enmity between
yourselves. Your dwelling-place and your means
of livelihood shall be on earth - for a time.' He
said: 'Therein shall you live, and therein shall
you die; but from it you shall be taken out (at
last).'   (Surah 7:19-25. See also 2:35-39).*

Thus far the Qur'an narrative agrees to a certain
extent with the narrative of the Bible. The resulting
theology drawn from the story, however, differs
absolutely, and is the cause of the gulf which divides
Muslim from Christian, (or, for that matter, Christian
from Jew). For both Muslims and Jews claim that
the Trinitarian theology of the Christian Church is
quite wrong, a terrible theological error, the sort of
'Baalism' against which the Blessed Jesus himself
(ﷺ) as a devoutly submitted Jew would have reacted
with horror.[4]

Christian theology teaches that the sin committed
by Adam and Eve (the Original Sin) was in some
way transmitted through them to all future human
beings. Since all future humanity was present in the
loins of Adam, it was passed on – as it were –
genetically. Every human child was therefore born
in sin and tainted by sin, and as this applied to

4.   See my book 'Have the Christians Got it All Wrong?'

every human, no human would ever have the power to be rid of it. Thus Christianity fell into the sin of 'shirk', meaning the 'division of the Godhead into partners' - following the Baalist tradition of 'inherited original sin' that needed an incarnate god-saviour-hero to rescue humanity. These theologies were common throughout the Mediterranean peoples, and the monotheistic prophets of the Bible struggled against their influence for the entire Biblical history. The main idea of Trinitarianism was to have a Supreme Father-God, and a human-virgin-born 'god-man' son, destined to die a sacrificial death in order to be resurrected to glory to save humanity. By identifying with the human race yet at the same time being much greater than it - the 'price paid' by the 'god-man' was a necessary sacrificial element in all Baalist and Trinitarian systems.

Islam, on the contrary, followed the teaching revealed to the noble Prophet Ezekiel (Nabi Dhulfikl (ﷺ)), that although an offspring might well suffer for the sins of the parents, God would never *punish* a child for the sins of the parent, but each individual would stand alone, and be judged on his or her own record alone.

The revelation of the Qur'an insists:

'Every soul draws the outcome of its acts upon none but itself; no bearer of burdens can bear

*the burden of another.' (Surah 6:164; see also
17:15; 29:13; 35:18; 39:7; 53:38).*

The following is a passage from Ezekiel's (☙)
book of prophecies in the Old Testament, a passage
which is virtually never expounded to Christian
children, for the obvious reason that it directly
opposes the doctrine of inherited original sin and
the need for a sacrificial redeemer. It is such an
important passage, and so consistently ignored by
Christians, that it is worth quoting in full. Muslims
will note that every word of it is completely in
keeping with the revelation of the Qur'an made
later to the Blessed Muhammad (☙). Here are
Ezekiel's (☙) words:

The Word of the Lord came to me again: 'What
do you mean by repeating this proverb concerning
the land of Israel - the fathers have eaten sour
grapes and the children's teeth are set on edge? As
I live', said the Lord God, 'this proverb shall no
more be used by you in Israel.

Behold, all souls are mine; the soul of the father
as well as the soul of the son is mine; the soul that
sins (and not someone else standing in for it) shall
die. If a person is righteous and does what is lawful
and right - if he does not eat upon the mountains
(i.e. worship idols) or lift up his eyes to the idols of
the house of Israel, does not defile his neighbour's
wife or approach a woman in her time of impurity,

does not oppress anyone but restores to the debtor his pledge, commits no robbery, gives his bread to the hungry and covers the naked with a garment, does not lend at interest or take any increase, withholds his hand from iniquity, executes true justice between man and man, walks in My statutes, and is careful to observe My commands - then he is righteous and he shall surely live,' says the Lord.

'If he begets a son who is a robber, a shedder of blood, who does none of these duties,.... that son shall not live. He has done all these abominable things; he shall surely die; his blood shall be upon himself.

But if a man begets a son who sees all the sins which his father has done, and has reverence for God, and does not do likewise.... he shall not die for his father's iniquity; he shall surely live....Yet you say: 'Why should the son not suffer for the sin of the father?' No, when that son has done what is lawful and right, and has been careful to observe all my statutes, he shall surely live. The soul that sins shall die. The son shall not suffer for the iniquity of the father, nor the father suffer for the iniquity of the son; the righteousness of the righteousness shall be upon himself, and the wickedness of the wicked shall be upon himself.

But if a wicked man turns away from all his sins which he has committed and (changes himself, and) keeps all my statutes and does what is lawful and right, he shall surely live; he shall not die. None of the transgressions which he has committed shall be remembered against him; he shall live because of the righteousness which he has done. Have I any pleasure in the death of the wicked?' says the Lord God, 'and not rather that he should turn from his way and live?' *(Ezekiel 18:1-23)*

Every Christian would do well to meditate upon that passage, and wonder why God revealed it to Ezekiel (ﷺ), with no hint of any Trinitarianism to come. If belief in an Atoning Saviour was necessary for salvation, then why did He deliberately mislead His followers? Both Jews and Muslims believe firmly that God never misleads:

'God will not mislead a people after He has guided them.' *(Surah 9:115)*

Now, the Qur'an does not follow up the story of the Fall of Adam and Eve by any attempt to record their history, but by the call to present-day humanity to learn from their example and not make the same mistakes.

'O children of Adam! We have bestowed raiment upon you to cover your shame, as well as to be an adornment of you. But the raiment of righteousness - that is the best. Such are among the signs of God, that they may receive admonition. O you children of Adam! Let not

*Shaytan reduce you in the same manner as he
got your parents out of the gardens, stripping
them of their raiment to expose their shame;
for he and his tribe watch you from a position
where you cannot see them. We made the evil
ones friends to those without faith. When they
do anything that is shameful, they say; 'We
found our fathers doing so', and 'God
commanded us thus'. Say: 'Nay, God never
commands what is shameful. Do you say of
God what you know not?' Say: 'My Lord has
commanded justice; and that you set your whole
selves (to Him) at every time and place of
prayer, and call upon Him, making your devotion
sincere as in His sight; (in that way) such as
He created you in the beginning, so shall you
return.'*   *(Surah 7:26-29)*

And what happened to the jinn? They carried on
existing, but the Qur'an is quite clear that so long
as humans stand firm in their faith in Allah, they
have nothing to fear from Shaytan or his evil spirits.

*'(God said), 'Lead to destruction those whom
you can! As for My servants, you shall have no
authority over them!'*   *(Surah 17:64)*[5]

The powers of evil are not equal to God. They

5.   (See also Surahs 2:34,36; 3:36; 4:117-120; 5:94; 7:11-18,
     200-201; 8:48; 14:22; 15:17; 31-44; 16;98-100; 17;61-65;
     18:50; 20:116-123; 22:52-53; 24:21; 35:6; 36:60; 38:71-85).

are very limited, and can always be overcome by the love of God. Humans who love and serve God are always more powerful than evil.

> *'Those who patiently persevere and seek God with regular prayers, and give generously - these overcome Evil with Good.'* *(Surah 13:22)*

The attitude of the Qur'an towards the jinn is actually completely true to the compassionate nature of Allah. It does not suggest that humans should automatically regard jinn as enemies and fight them. No, humans are to recognise that jinn are also creations of Allah, and should be treated with sympathy. Although some have descended to evil and trickery, this is not the case for all of them, by any means. Jinn, like humans have free-will - unlike the angels, and are able to hear the Message just as well as humans, and choose to either accept or reject it.

One Surah of the Qur'an (Surah 72) is specifically entitled 'The Jinn', and tells of the seven jinn of Nakhlah who heard and obeyed the Qur'an.

> *'A company of jinns listened to the Qur'an. They said, 'We have heard a wonderful recital. It gives guidance to the right, and we have believed in it. We shall not join any gods with our Lord. Exalted is the Majesty of our Lord -*

He has taken neither a wife nor a son. There
were some foolish ones among us, who used to
utter extravagant lies against God; but we
think that no human or spirit should say anything
that is untrue against God.'   *(Surah 72:1-5)*

It was in grappling with the doctrine of Original
Sin that the Christian Church fell into the sin of
shirk.

Not all Christian theologians agreed with
Trinitarianism, as it happened. Pelagius, for example,
was condemned as a heretic when he questioned the
truth of the original sin being transmitted to all the
future descendants of Adam. He believed the Islamic
doctrine that every individual person could choose
to act rightly through his or her own moral will, and
would then be 'saved' and earn the reward of going
to Paradise.

As the Christian belief in Adam and Eve began to
fade, scientific thinkers tried to find other ways
round the problem of moral evil. The philosopher
John Locke, for example, thought that perhaps God
had implanted certain desires in people, and we had
to use our wills to decide whether or not we would
satisfy them. Thomas Hume went further, and
considered that Man's behaviour was the inevitable
result of the character he was born with, and he
could not be held responsible for that himself. If a

person's character was altered, by tampering with the brain, for example, then he would act in a different manner. These ideas were picked up in the twentieth century by those who thought it would be a good idea to change the character of our thugs and murderers by brain surgery - the infamous frontal lobotomy experiments.

Muslims believe that the universe is permeated by both positive and antagonistic energies, and the more a person seeks to serve God, the more they become aware of this tension. If good is amplified in a person, so are other things like selfishness, lust, the urge for personal prestige and power. It is out of his tension, and mental and spiritual jihad (striving) to recognise and do the will of God, that growth and further creativity become possible.

Striving against the 'evil' brings about changes in our level of consciousness. Experiencing evil and suffering produces real maturation, and real command of life. The Muslim has to rechannel what was learned from the evil into new and vital energies.

CHAPTER SIX

ARE WE PREDESTINED?

Many people believe that our future, from the day of our birth to the day of our death, and indeed even our fates after death, are somehow written in advance. This it is not uncommon for a Muslim to say when calamity strikes – 'Mektub', 'it is written'. Some Muslims , indeed, believe that Allah controls us absolutely, our fates being written on 'tablets of destiny'[6], and that by divine decree before humans are born, Allah determines all that will happen to people, including the length of their life, whether they will be male or female, rich or poor, healthy or sick, miserable or happy, and so on. It all exists in God's 'mind', or in our 'books', before it comes to pass.

This inevitably leads to the belief that since God knows everything beforehand, He must also determine

---

6   This is not the same as the belief in the eternal existence of the full text of the written Qur'an, which was shown to the Prophet (pbuh) on the Night of Power, before being revealed over 23 years, section by section.

who will obey Him and who will disobey, and so even before a person is born, God has already determined whether he or she is destined for everlasting life in Paradise or doomed to everlasting Hell.

It is the very opposite of believing in chance. Belief in fate, or destiny, is one of the oldest and most widespread of religious beliefs, to explain all that is inexplicable in our existence. We often hear people say: 'It was obviously not his time to die', or 'That's the way it was meant to be'. Fate basically conveys the idea that everything that happens, every event – whether good or bad – is inevitable; it is destined to occur because it has been determined in advance by a higher force beyond the control of Man.

The English word 'fate' comes from the Latin *fatum*, meaning 'a prophetic declaration, an oracle, a divine determination.' An atheist scientist might perhaps think some random force determines our futures in an unavoidable and inexplicable way, but most people think of this force as being God – a 'Higher Power' controlling and directing our affairs, shaping the lives of individuals and nations in advance, and making the future just as inevitable as the past.

Belief in predestination – whether or not there is such a thing – can certainly determine how we act.

Many people passively accept their situation, however unjust or oppressive, as though it were their unchangeable lot in life, because 'it must be God's will'. In this way, belief in fate can undermine the notion of personal responsibility, and instead promote carelessness and laziness. A healthy sense of personal responsibility is important. It is one of the things that motivates parents to provide for their families, workers to perform their tasks conscientiously, manufacturers to produce quality products. Belief in fate numbs that sense. If a man knows there is a fault in his car and has a keen sense of responsibility, he will have it repaired out of concern for the lives of his passengers. A believer in fate might just ignore the risk, reasoning that an accident or breakdown will occur only if it is 'God's will'.

Belief in fate can also result in another character trait - some very false self-congratulation. Success in business and the accumulation of wealth were often seen as signs of God's favour, and thus God's blessing could be claimed for some very suspect activity indeed. If rich crooks got away with it, they must have believed that their gods shaped their destinies as well as those of all humanity, individually and collectively; the gods in control of the cosmos therefore planned and instituted evil, falsehood and violence as part and parcel of their civilisation.

Another very widespread belief was that it was

possible to find out their gods' plans through divination – a technique of communicating with these gods. This involved trying to foretell the future by observing, deciphering and interpreting such things as dreams, astrology, palms of hands, bumps on heads, the casting of lots, animal behaviour and entrails. Evidence for this can be found however far back we search, in Mesopotamia, Egypt and elsewhere. In fact, divination seems to have been an integral part of life. Casting lots was supposed to eliminate the possibility of human manipulation and thereby give the gods a clear channel through which to express their wishes.

However, the gods' wishes were not always inexorable – sometimes appeals and appropriate sacrifices could avert an evil future. And there were always unscrupulous people who could use the notion of fate for more sinister purposes, and especially to help subdue the masses. The belief that the universe was governed by Fate would have special appeal to the ruling classes – it gave them a built-in justification for the fixed order, in other words, ruthless self-interest.

Events or things used to predict the future were called *portenta* or 'signs'. The messages given were called *omina* (from which we obviously get the word *ominous*). Greeks and Romans used oracles and mediums widely, believing this was how the gods communicated with humans. The result was fear, rather than hope. The purpose of life became the escape of misfortune rather than the desire to achieve good.

Allah's ability to know everything in advance, and guide everything by His power is clearly stated in the Qur'an and the Bible. Indeed, divine foreknowledge and foreordination form the basis for all true prophecy. The whole point of prophecy was that God communicated with humanity by means of either spoken or written word, delivered through His spokesmen, the prophets. These writings still exist for us to examine, and see what they reveal about God's prophecies, such things as the fall of Babylon, the rebuilding of Jerusalem, the rise and fall of various monarchs and kingdoms.[7] The Prophet Daniel insisted that the the fulfilment of such prophecies was one of the strongest proofs that the Scriptures were indeed God's Word. Isaiah reveals God stating: 'I am the Divine One, and there is no other God, nor anyone like Me; the One telling from the beginning the finale, and from long ago the things that have not yet been done; the One saying – 'My Own counsel will stand, and everything that is My delight, I shall do... I have spoken it; I shall bring it to pass. I have conceived it, I shall also perform it.'[8]

7.   See, for example, Isaiah 13:17-19; 44:24-45:1.
8.   Isaiah 46:9-11; 55:10-11.

In the Qur'an Allah challenges all who believe in other gods to furnish proof for their claims by foretelling similar acts of salvation and judgement, and then bringing them to pass. Their impotence in this respect demonstrates that their idols are nothing but fantasies and unreality. The Hebrew name by which the Prophets knew Allah was 'Jehovah' or 'Yahweh', which literally means 'He causes to become.'[9]

However, the most important factor to be considered is that Allah created human beings as free moral agents. People are intended to be the Khalifahs of Allah[10], His deputies on earth, and He endowed them with the privilege and responsibility of free choice, thereby making them accountable for their own acts. Therefore, logically, there should be no conflict between God's foreknowledge and the free moral agency of His intelligent creatures. Thus, Allah not only uses His power of foreknowledge in the working out of His purposes, He has often used it to warn the wicked of their impending judgement as well as to give His servants hope of salvation.

The third factor is that of Allah's own moral standards and qualities, as revealed in the words of

---

9.   Genesis 12:7-8; Exodus 3:13-15; Psalm 83:18.

10. The word *khalifah* means someone delegated to be responsible on behalf of another, in this case, human beings being responsible for the planet on behalf of its Creator, Allah.

the Holy Book, and though His 'Beautiful Names'.
God's 'names' are not names, but qualities. They
include justice, honesty, impartiality, love, mercy
and kindness. If predestination was reality, we would
have to imagine God organising – 'today Husayn
will be injured in a car accident, Hannah will catch
malaria, Ahmad's house and fields will be wiped
out in a hurricane, etc'. God may *know* these things,
but what are we saying about Him if we believe He
arbitrarily *causes* these unpleasant things for us?

The important thing to try to get our minds
around is whether or not Allah's exercise of His
foreknowledge is, like Himself, infinite - without
limit? Does He foresee and foreknow all future
actions of all His created beings, whether human,
spirit or animal? Does He fore-ordain such actions,
or even predestine the final destiny of all the creatures,
even doing so before they have come into existence?
If God does fully and infinitely exercise His
foreknowledge, and does indeed fore-ordain the course
and destiny of all individuals this directly *conflicts*
with the doctrine of freewill, which Allah stated He
world confer upon sentient beings.

If God is All-knowing, of course He must know
not only past and present, but also the future. Those
who believe in predestination argue that if God did
not foreknow all matters in their minutest detail, He

would not be perfect as regards knowledge. They believe that God foreknows and fore-ordains the future of all His creatures not just from their birth, not just from their conception in the womb, but from before creation even began.

St. Augustine rejected the 'false and noxious opinions' of astrologers, and argued that 'to confess that God exists, and at the same time to deny that He has foreknowledge of future things, is the most manifest folly.' He claimed that for God to be truly almighty, He must 'know all things before they come to pass', leaving nothing unordained.[11]

Many centuries later, the foremost Protestant proponent of predestination was the French Reformer, John Calvin[12]. He defined predestination as 'the eternal decree of God, by which he determined what He wanted to do with each person.' Since God knew everything, He must therefore know who would be saved and who he damned even before the individuals were born. 'All people were not created in the same condition, but eternal life was fore-ordained for some, and eternal damnation for others.' He also asserted: 'God not only foresaw the fall of the first man, Adam, and in him the ruin of his posterity; but also, at His own pleasure, *arranged* it.' Others attacked this very rigid determinism by

11. St Augustine – 'The City of God', Book V, chapters 7-9.
12. In the sixteenth century.

pointing out that the religious writings often mentioned freewill, and that humans must be free to choose and act, since God, Who is Perfect Justice, holds them responsible and accountable for their actions.

So, prior to creating man, jinn or angel, did God exercise His powers of foreknowledge and knew everything that would result from such creation? Did He know the jinn Iblis (Shaytan) would rebel against Him, with the subsequent rebellion of the first human couple, and all the unfolding consequences right down to and beyond the present day?

Many Muslims, and other People of the Book, in accepting the omnipotence and omniscience of God, do accept that this must be so, and that it is a meritorious thing to have this faith.

Others, however, feel the strong concern that this makes the whole business of the existence of things other than God and the concept of Judgement absolutely pointless. *Why* should God wish to do this? If He knew the end from the beginning, then surely He foreknew all about humanity's fall into sin and the disastrous consequences this would bring. If God has foreseen and decreed the course and destiny of every human, can it truly be said that we are free to choose our life's course?

Is it possible that instead of 'knowing everything', God chooses to be selective and discretionary in

His foreknowledge, so that He himself makes the decision how much He wishes to foresee and foreknow? The Holy Books reveal that God *has* given to each person the freewill to choose which destiny they will get. As the prophet Musa/Moses (ﷺ) declared to the Banu Israil: God said – 'I have put life and death before you...you must choose life in order that you may live, you and your offspring, by loving the Lord your God and by sticking to Him; for He is your life and the length of your days.'[13]

The prophet Isa/Jesus (ﷺ) pointed out: 'Go in through the narrow gate, because the road is broad and spacious that leads to destruction, and many are those who go in through it; whereas narrow is the gate and cramped the road leading to life, and few are those who find it.'[14]

In other words, two roads, two destinies; our future becomes contingent upon our choices and actions. To obey God means life, and to disobey and reject Him, death.

If this is so, then instead of preceding our existence, God's determination of our eternal destinies could then logically await His judgement on the *actual* course and actions of our lives, and of our proven attitudes under test. That would give a great deal

13. Deuteronomy 30:19-20.
14. St Matthew's Gospel 7:13-14.

more point to the tests, and to the notion that Messengers could be sent from God in order that human beings might change their lives and beliefs by listening to what they had to say.

The major problem and consequence of the predestination concept is that it does not harmonize with the stated standards, qualities and purposes of God as revealed by His Messengers, either those in the Bible or the Prophet of Islam (ﷺ). If every detail was predestined, it necessarily means that all the wickedness, crime, immorality, oppression, tyranny and hypocrisy also existed in the mind of God before creation's beginning.

And if the Creator had indeed exercised His power to foreknow all that has taken place since the beginning of history, then the full weight of all that wickedness must have been deliberately set in motion by God Himself - which surely brings into question the reasonableness and consistency of the whole concept of predestination, or the Justice of God's Judgement.

Despite being surrounded by nations with a fatalistic view of life, the Prophets of the One True God insisted throughout the Old Testament that people should reject fatalism. Divination and sorcery was forbidden, on pain of death. They taught that humanity and the world were certainly not the prey of some blind force, but that God had a purpose for them. They were not intended to just sit back and let things happen, but on the contrary, to 'do all that your hand finds to do, with all your power,' (Ecclesiastes 9:10). Central to this was the concept of their freewill. They were free to choose whether to serve God or not, and thus shape their own futures. God said: 'Look – I put before you life and good, and death and bad.' (Deuteronomy 30:15). Each person's future was dependent on his or her own actions and decisions.

Let us try to come at this from a different angle. Does perfection really demand such an absolute all-embracing definition? Would God really be imperfect if He did not foreknow everything in each specific detail?

Surely one could argue that God is undeniably 'perfect' in might and power, and infinite in capacity, but He is not required to use His power to the full extent of His omnipotence? The evidence of history, is it stands, certainly suggests that God does not always use His powers. It may indeed be true that God's might and judgement destroyed the people in the time of Nuh/Noah (عليه السلام), wiped out Sodom and Gomorrah in the time of Lut/Lot (عليه السلام). He destroyed many ancient cities and nations - but there are a whole lot of equally wicked and decadent societies still thriving on whom God has chosen to show mercy, or at least a time of respite. This suggests that God certainly chooses to exercise His infinite ability of justice and foreknowledge in a selective way, to the extent that is His will.

Therefore, it is surely not a question of God's ability to foresee, foreknow, foreordain, for all things are possible to God. The question is rather God's will - *what* He chooses to foreordain! The alternative to predestination is that Allah is selective, uses His own discretion, but in a way that harmonizes with the standards and is consistent with that He reveals of Himself. He examines a situation, considers, knows, and then He comes to decision.

If this is so, it means that Allah could with all sincerity set before humans the prospect and possibility of life genuinely free from wickedness, rather than all of history from creation onwards just being a rerun of what had already been foreordained.

After all, to offer something very desirable to us unfortunate human beings on conditions known beforehand to be unreachable is surely both hypocritical and cruel - not qualities we associate with God at all. God's word presents the prospect of everlasting life in paradise as a goal it *is* possible for all humans to attain. Mortals are urged to reject the bad, and turn to the good; to accept the will of God, do it, to turn away from transgression and achieve paradise. Logically, why should Allah do this if He foreknew that certain of these individuals being thus exhorted were predestined to die in wickedness? The message is surely to turn and be saved.

Allah is patient and does not desire any person to be destroyed. If He already foreknew and fore-ordained which individuals would receive eternal salvation, and which would receive eternal destruction, it may well be asked what is the possible meaning of such 'patience', and how sincere is God's desire that all should be saved? The desire is then totally meaningless. We do not believe God to be such a hypocrite - the characteristics of love towards us and hope for our well-being are what we have been led to expect. Allah wishes us all to gain salvation, unless we insist on proving ourselves unworthy and beyond hope.

We can see from the amazing complexities of the laws of the universe, and the intricate design of things within it, the brilliance and intelligence of our Designer, who moves everything towards the accomplishment of His divine will. Just because humans are granted freewill, it does not mean that things will always be broken or wasted through lack of foresight, or that God must continually be putting His system right as it goes out of order.

Moreover, God can certainly know the course that certain groups or nations will take - but this knowledge does not deprive individuals within such groups exercising their free choice as to which course they will follow - as for example in Noah's (ﷺ) escape from the destruction of his neighbours.

God tests individuals by causing or allowing certain circumstances or events, or by causing individuals to hear His inspired messages - the point of which is that they are then obliged to exercise their free choice to make a decision, and thus reveal a particular attitude of heart.

According to the way they respond, Allah can mould them in the course they have selected of their own volition. Thus, the heart must 'incline' the foot towards a certain way, and then Allah can direct the steps.

> *'God does not change human beings until they change what is in themselves.' (Surah 13:11).*

Under testing, one's heart can become fixed - either hardened in wrongdoing, rebellion, bitterness, or made true in unbreakable devotion. Having reached such a point of his and her own choice, the end result of an individual's course can now be foreknown, and foretold with no injustice or violation of that human's free moral agency.

CHAPTER SEVEN

FACING THE TESTS

What kinds of things are evil? (We must remember that we are thinking in relative terms - things that seem evil to us). It seems that there are two main sorts, physical and moral evil. Physical evil is suffering which arises from natural causes like floods, earthquakes, diseases, and so on, and we can perhaps accept that these are totally locked into the working out of Natural Law, cause and effect. Floods, storms, earthquakes are often called 'acts of God' on insurance policies. Yet the revelations do not suggest that God really causes natural disasters in order to punish us.

Many people experience an awareness of God in the beauties of Nature - things like the blossoms of spring and the glorious sunset; and they often forget that Nature is not calm and gentle and peaceful at all. It is 'red in tooth and claw'. Really, we seem to exist in spite of Nature. Nature cares nothing at all for those it wipes out. It does not discriminate. A landslide would just as soon fall on masses of innocent children as on one villain.

The cosmos must be governed by regular laws, and it is hard to see how these regularities could be adapted to the changing desires and predicaments of sentient beings; when 'plasticity of behaviour' characterises conscious beings it is inevitable that there will every so often be 'collisions' between these beings and their regular environment. If the regular laws kept changing to accommodate all our mishaps, there would be chaos.

This is relevant to a further point. It is hard to see how pain and suffering could be eliminated if there are to be evolving conscious beings. The regularities in our background teach us intelligence, prudence, how to estimate probabilities and develop rational behaviour and morality. A random and haphazard world could not develop rational and moral beings. As it is, human beings have to painfully learn through errors, and observing misfortunes, how to acquire skills and moral attributes such as compassion, unselfishness and self-sacrifice.

Nature is governed by rules which do not change and alter to suit our convenience. The same rules apply when we humans act in Nature - if we bomb people with napalm, then they are burnt. Bullets kill, drunken driving kills, carelessness in industry and in the home kills. These things cause untold suffering - but are they really God's fault? Isn't it rather unfair to expect God to intervene and break the Laws of Nature on our behalf when we set something in motion? It is our business to live within these laws, and use them for the benefits of humanity. If we pollute our atmosphere or destroy our children, the responsibility is surely ours.

In reality, *people* are often to blame when things go wrong. Failures at school, at work or in social relations such as marriage may result from a lack of effort or training, or consideration for others. Likewise, illnesses, accidents and deaths might be the result of negligence. Thus, wearing a seat-belt dramatically reduces the likelihood of being killed in a car accident – which would obviously make no difference if unalterable 'fate' were at work. Proper medical care and sanitation also greatly reduce the number of premature deaths. Many of the so-called 'acts of God' disasters are also really the sad legacy of our ignorance and mismanagement of the earth and its resources. Many attract disaster when they 'reap what they sow'; countless millions live in poverty because they are victimized by greedy people in power.

Moral evil is certainly the result of our actions - not the bad things that we do through ignorance, but deliberate unkind and malicious actions. Moral evil arises through deliberate negligence, selfishness, hatred and spite. However, if God created the universe, we are still entitled to be baffled by the fact that He allows so much badness to arise and go unchecked in conscious beings.

One of the things most difficult to reconcile with the belief that God is supposed to know the exact span of our lifetimes, the exact second of our death, is the fact that some people commit murder, or suicide. When someone kills, have they *altered* a fixed fate, or have they been *used* by God to bring about someone else's fate?

It is important here to keep in mind the distinction between dying and killing. You cannot choose the moment of your own death, but you *can* choose to kill.

When a creature dies in natural circumstances, when its 'time has come', Islam teaches that its soul is separated from its body by the angel of death, Israfil. The body then begins to disintegrate into the various component atomic parts of which it was made. It 'goes back to dust'. It doesn't make any difference whether the body is buried, cremated, exploded, burnt, eaten by fishes or vultures. The body rots away, or is absorbed into something else, while the soul waits for the Day of Resurrection when it will be reunited with its body created anew, and face the Judgement to come. Muslims believe that if the person has been wicked or cruel, they will suffer torment and constriction 'in the grave', whereas for the souls of those who have succeeded in being good in their lives the 'graves are expanded' to limiltless distances, and they can have all sorts of experiences.

A person cannot decide: 'I think I will die tomorrow', and then sit back and die. The time of that person's death is fixed and known to Allah, and they cannot bring hold it back for one second, however much they would wish to cling on to it, perhaps for unfinished business, or out of fear; neither can they bring it forward by one second, however much they might wish to because they are perhaps in great pain, or have become 'living vegetables', or are so depressed and sick of life they want to escape from it.

> *'To every people is a term appointed; when their term is reached, not an hour can they cause delay; nor an hour can they advance (it in anticipation).* (Surah 7:34)

However, people *do* have the freewill to decide if they will kill or not, whether killing some other person or animal, or their own selves. When a person kills, it is not a case of a soul gently leaving a body, but of the body being attacked and the soul *forced* out. The physical body is harmed to such an extent that it becomes impossible for that body to sustain life – for example, the killer stabs a vital organ or poisons a vital system. In these cases, the victims killed have not died when Allah intended them to die, but the freewill of the killer has intervened.

This can only happen by God's leave and with His knowledge; it must therefore mean that God has in fact willed that the human malevolent will is allowed to take precedence in the time and sphere of human existence.

God's foreknowledge is rather like that of a supreme computer that knows all the eventualities. If so-and-so does *this*, then *that* will happen. On the other hand, if he chooses this *other* course, then *another* thing will happen. If that person with overpowering rage slams out of his house, and into his car, then that person driving along in his way to the city may be crashed into and die, and so might some innocent bystanders. However, if he chooses to take some medicine that will calm him down, he may instead rest until his temper is under control once more, and none of these things will happen.

Muslims are aware of a dimension to the purpose of evil that is completely in keeping with the will of

God, and to which it is their duty to submit. Muslims do not just pass their lives without bearing in mind the eternal consequences of their intentions and actions. They believe God's statement that everything they do and think is known to Him - every thought, every inclination, every motive.

> *'Allah has full knowledge of the secrets of your hearts and is fully aware of all that you do.'*   *(Surah 5:7-8; 2.231)*

Islam teaches that the reason for living is not just to wander aimlessly about, enjoying yourself and avoiding pain and evil as best you can. It is to pass a test. Therefore, it stands to reason that not every part of our lives is going to be pleasant or easy. Tests never are. We are inevitably going to be confronted with things that will hurt us, or cause us despair. It is not possible for any human being to pass their lifetime without coming up against these times of testing - so they might as well reconcile themselves to that fact straight away, rather than waste time wondering why 'this has happened to me?'

> *'If a wound has touched you, be sure a similar wound has touched others. Such days (of varying fortunes) We give to men and men by turns: that Allah may know those that believe, and that He may take to Himself from your ranks martyr-witnesses.'*   *(Surah 3:140)*

'You shall certainly be tried and tested in your
possessions and in your personal selves; and
you shall certainly hear much that will grieve
you from those who received the Book before
you, and from those who worship many gods.
But if you persevere patiently and guard against
evil - then that will be the determining factor
in all affairs.'   *(Surah 3:186)*

If we were just being spied on by a Know-All God for the sole purpose of bringing us down, then our Lord would not be the Compassionate, the Merciful, but some kind of malicious despot, laughing at our troubles and enjoying the spectacle of seeing us get into difficulties. We do not admire our fellow-humans when they act like this; and if they are in a position to hurt and punish us for the things we get wrong, we consider them to be despicable tyrants against whom it would be perfectly justifiable to rebel.

It would hardly be responsible for God to place us in situations which are intolerable for us and then expect us to be successful. That would make Him God the Very Unfair. No, He has promised that no matter how dreadful our circumstances might seem, He will not burden us with any trial that is really beyond our capacity to bear. One of the Muslim acts of faith is this trust in God, that He knows all the things that we are going through, and will never desert us.

> *'On no soul does God place a burden greater than it can bear. Before Us is a record which clearly shows the truth. They will never be wronged.'*   *(Surah 23:62)*

Therefore, the tests and trials of confronting evil are not unreasonable, even if we may think they are at the time we are going through them.

> *'Be sure that We shall test you with something of fear and hunger, some loss in goods or lives or the fruits of your toil; but give glad tidings to those who patiently persevere, who say, when afflicted by calamity - 'To God we belong, and to Him is our return.'*
>
> *(Surah 2:155-156)*

If one has this trust, one's whole attitude to calamity is changed. We can be grateful for the good times, thankful when everything is going well and we are successful, healthy and happy; but we should be alert in the knowledge that tests are bound to come upon us, and we can recognise them and deal with them when they do.

> 'At evening, do not expect to live till morning; at morning, do not expect to live till evening. Take from your health for your sickness, and from your life for your death.'   *(Muslim)*

One basic difference between the Muslim attitude to natural but 'untimely' death as opposed to 'killing'and that of the Christian, is that the Muslim cannot regard it as 'untimely'. If it happened, then it must have been God's will, for Muslims believe that our days are numbered from the time we are conceived in the womb. This means that when such a natural death occurs, the Muslim does not tend to lose faith in God, or find his or her confidence in God shaken.

'Nor can a soul die expect by God's leave, the term being fixed as by writing. If any do desire a reward in this life We shall give it to him; and if any do desire a reward in the Hereafter, We shall give it to him. And swiftly shall We reward those that (serve Us with) gratitude.'
(Surah 3:146)

Muslims accept that death comes to all, at such a time as God wills. Our attitude to death is but one of our tests; the true Muslim submits everything to God, including the offering up of life itself.

'How can you reject faith in God? Seeing that you were without life and He gave you life; then He will cause you to die, and will again bring you to life; and again to Him will you return.'   *(Surah 2:28)*

Histrionics and excessive grief are out of place -

although Muslims are just as sad to lose their loved ones as anyone else, the true Muslim attitude is one of trustful acceptance.

The hadiths give us the moving example of the death of the son of Umm Sulaym and Abu Talhah:

Anas b. Malik (the stepson of Abu Talhah) reported that while Abu Talhah was on a journey his son breathed his last. When Abu Talhah came back, he said to his wife: 'What news about my child?' Umm Sulaym said: 'He is now in a more comfortable state than before.' She served him the evening meal, and he took it. He then came to her (and was intimate with her), and when only the next morning, when it was all over, did she tell him about the little boy's death. She said: 'If someone had left something valuable with you, and then gone on a journey, and eventually returned and asked for you to give back that valuable thing, would you hold it back from him?' He said: 'No.' Then she told him what had happened and asked him to make arrangements for the burial of the child. Abu Talhah went to Allah's Messenger (ﷺ) and informed him, whereupon he said: 'Did you spend the night with her?' He said: 'Yes'. The Blessed Prophet then said: 'O Allah bless both of them.' And in due course she gave birth to another child.' *(Hadith Muslim)*

People have even been saved from suicidal despair

by having understanding of the tests revealed to them. Some stretches in people's lives are so terrible, one bad thing happening after another. Stress causes misfortunes to zoom in on us. However, if we regard the latest misfortune as just another test to be dealt with, and have trust in the knowledge that we are credited with our successes of coping (even if no-one on earth credits us with them!), it enables us to 'hang on in there', and come through the 'dark valley'.

> *'Be firm and patient and in pain (or suffering) and adversity, and throughout all periods of panic. Such are the people of truth, the God-fearing.'*   *(Surah 2:177)*

Why does God want to test us? It is because from these tests we grow out of weakness and selfishness, and become strong, understanding, compassionate and faithful people. Sometimes, the suffering and pain that burden the dark events of our life, such as severe illness, redundancy, bereavement or betrayal, can be authentic healing agents in their own right. Anything that deflects a person from a previously heedless way of life and causes him or her to think about the deeper issues of existence, perhaps for an the first time in his or her earthly career, is potentially an agent of healing. Sometimes, we have to descend a considerable distance down the pit of despair before we can find true healing of our souls.

'That which is on earth We have made but as a glittering show, in order that We may test them - as to which of them are best in conduct.'
(*Surah 18:7*)

There is a story about a farmer in Africa who grew hemp to make strong rope. He had to grow it in terrible conditions, back-breaking soil with little rain to nourish it. When he moved to a place with a more easy-going climate he took some hemp plants with him, thinking how lovely they would grow in these conditions. Yes, they grew - huge lush green plants. But when he opened up the stems to take out the fibre - there was nothing there but pulp. The hemp *needed* the harsh conditions in which to develop 'backbone'. So, the true Muslim learns to accept, to thank God, even for the harsh conditions.

'And We shall try you, until We test those among you who strive their utmost and persevere in patience; and We shall try your reported mettle.' (*Surah 47:31*)

'Nothing shall be accounted to humanity but what they have striven for.' (*Surah 53:39*)

'Those who strive hard in Our way - surely We shall guide them on to Our paths.'
(*Surah 29:68*)

The purpose of the Muslim life is, therefore, to

face all the tests that come our way, and always strive to live in God's way, no matter how difficult. People without awareness of God live only on the level of animals - eating drinking, procreating, suffering and dying. Really, there is little point to their lives, as they themselves will often admit, especially when things go wrong and they get depressed. But those who have awareness of God are also aware of eternity, and their sufferings are meaningful.

> *'Do you think you will enter Paradise without God establishing which of you have struggled hard and who have been patient?*
>
> *(Surah 3:142)*

> *'Do people really think that if they (merely) say 'We believe' they will be left to themselves and not put to the test? We certainly put to the test all that came before them.'*
>
> *(Surah 29:2-3)*

Let us close this chapter with the beautiful final words of Surah al-Baqarah:

> *'On no soul does God place a burden greater than it can bear. It gets every good that it earns and it suffers every ill that it earns. Pray: 'Our Lord! Do not condemn us if we forget or fall into error. Our Lord! Do not lay on us a burden like that which You laid on*

those who went before us. Our Lord! Do not lay on us a burden greater than we have the strength to bear. Blot out our sins and grant us forgiveness. Have mercy on us. You are our Protector; help us against those who stand against Faith.' (Surah 2:286)

Human beings do have freewill, and Allah, in bestowing this freedom, would be grossly inconsistent if He were forever interfering with it to prevent particular evils. And what would the freedom to only do good amount to? If there is a temptation which I have no chance of falling for because of my constitution, how can it really be called a temptation? Those who had been programmed so that they could never choose evil would be harmless, but could they really be called 'good'? Their goodness would be of no credit to them - praise and blame would not come into it.

One cannot just implant morality or creativity or rationality in a person. You cannot pump in enlightenment or conscience. It can only be drawn forth from an individual, by guidance as from a teacher, who stands back and lets the student make his or her own mistakes. There is no virtue in brain-washing the individual and calling this responsible morality. The person must see the goodness of virtue, and want it for himself and herself.

In the Middle Ages, the monk Abelard argued (also on Islamic lines) that the moral evil of an act was not the act itself, but the intention (niyyah) of the person who committed it. God would not judge what was done, but the reason why it was done. A sinful person was one who had deliberately chosen and set out to do wrong, and not, for example, someone who had done a dreadful thing but whose mind was sick or disturbed.

The hadiths of the Blessed Muhammad illustrate the importance of right intention, and also of actually doing the good thing; and wrong intention, but also of actually not doing what one was tempted to do.

Abu Hurayrah reported that the Messenger of Allah (ﷺ) observed: Allah, the Great and Glorious, said: 'Whenever my servant intends to do good, but does not do it, I (nevertheless) write one good act for him; but if he puts it into practice I write from ten to seven hundred good deeds in his favour. When he intends to commit an evil, but does not actually do it, I do not record it. But if he does it, I write only one evil.'   (*Hadith Muslim 234*)

St. Thomas Aquinas agreed with this principle, and pointed out another Islamic teaching - that as far as good actions were concerned, they could not be counted as good at all unless there was a deliberate intention to do good behind the deed. If a person's action 'just happened to be good' or beneficial, then there was no particular intention there, and it was not an act of free will at all, and no reward was merited.

Aquinas, however, differed from the Islamic dogma that each individual was responsible for his or her own sins, and thought that Adam's sin was transmittable to all future humanity, and that only God's grace and not human effort could save people - but although God's grace was always available, it was put to the individual to respond to it and accept it. God stood at the door and knocked; He did not barge in, or force people to believe in Him.

Therefore, Allah does not simply impose goodness on us. In creating us with freewill He is in a way limiting Himself; although He can continue to guide through various means (such as the Messages and the Holy Books), He does, to a great extent, leave His created being to their own devices.

Only on the soil of evil can good grow. People are responsible, for they are free - but their freedom implies that as the price there must be evil. So, then, are humans to be blamed for what could not be avoided? And is it just that any individual might be tortured or raped or driven mad, so that the race as a whole might develop towards being capable of marvellous things!

The highest expressions of human morality point out the claims and worth of each and every individual. So, if we argue that for the growth of morality and creativity, it may be necessary for individuals to be hurt and destroyed, it sounds too contradictory to be acceptable. Surely the innocent victim is entitled to protest?

Such a victim might well cry out and accuse God of callousness and injustice. However, if in submission to the will of God, the victim can substitute a new moral attitude for the sense of injustice at his or her suffering, then perhaps the will of God really may be done. If the victim can accept that the persecutors really do not know what they do, then the victim can also perhaps accept the role of a sacrifice or a martyr in the cause of progress. The evil that is done actually teaches others the tenable truth of what freedom means.

CHAPTER EIGHT

THE FORGIVENESS OF GOD

So, where does this leave our image of God? What is the test about, and why do any people get punished at all?

In fact, the Qur'an reveals two things; firstly, that God is not a wishy-washy accepter of any kind of conduct or morality, who will ignore the activities of people who deliberately and callously hurt and damage others, or who live egotistical selfish lives; and secondly, that it is not really God who punishes these people, but they bring it upon themselves.

'Allah is strict in punishment.'
(Surah 2:196; 5:3)

'Man is evidence against himself, even though he puts forward excuses.' *(Surah 75:14-15)*

Although God will in due course be obliged to punish certain people, it is never His will to be obliged to punish them. There is no divine satisfaction in surveying the baneful effects of sin; on the contrary, it is God's will that all evil should be healed. The Qur'an teaches that anyone who repents and turns back to God and makes some effort to put right the things they have done wrong, finds forgiveness straight away.

Nobody is perfect, we have all done things of which we were ashamed. If God punished us according to what we really deserved, then no-one would be left alive.

> *'If Allah were to punish people according to what they deserve, He would not leave on the earth a single living creature; but He gives them respite for a stated term; when their term expires, truly Allah has in His sights all His servants.'*   *(Surah 35:45)*

So, the Qur'an teaches that people who return to God need not grieve or fear, or despair of God's forgiveness for anything they did wrong; but those who insist on turning their backs on Him and behaving badly will be responsible for punishing themselves.

> *'If any one does evil or wrongs his own soul but afterwards seeks Allah's forgiveness, he will find Allah Oft-Forgiving, Most Merciful.'*
> *(Surah 4:110)*

> *'God is not unjust to them; (it is) they (who) are unjust to themselves.'*   *(Surah 3:117)*

Unfortunately, if God is not to remove evil from our universe, the consequences of this are very serious for us. We have freewill to decide whether or not we will be evil, and we have to decide what to do about people who are.

If humans have consciences, this must mean that from time to time we are presented with a choice of what to do over a given situation, and that our course of action will earn more respect in the eyes of ourselves and others than the other course of action. We can choose whether to gratify ourselves, or put other people before ourselves. If we put ourselves first when we know we should not have done, our consciences will trouble us, and we will feel ashamed. If we take revenge when we should have had compassion, we will feel ashamed.

Being Muslim implies doing what we ought to do, and what we ought to do should be fairly obvious to anyone in full possession of their senses.

Some, no doubt, will argue that no one ever is in full possession of their senses - we are programmed by our education and environment, and we are born with a set genetic make-up that will guarantee that we act in certain ways. But may be it is taking rather a lot for granted to suppose that there is nothing we can do to take charge of our own lives.

In one of the Blessed Jesus' (ﷺ) most famous

parables (The Parable of the Talents - St. Matthew's Gospel 25:13-30), he pointed out that God was a 'hard taskmaster', who expected back more than He gave out. The most important thing we have in this life is our potential. We can go forward, or we can throw everything away. No one can make us - the choice is ours.

God won't hold it against us if we are not very intelligent - we can't help the amount of brain we were born with - but we deserve to be held to blame if we have been lazy or selfish or unkind. Just saying that we believe in God is not good enough. Our lives must show that our belief has had an effect on us.

Abu Wail recorded : 'Truly, there are people who recite the Qur'an but it does not go down beyond their collar bones. It is beneficial only when it settles in the heart and is rooted deeply in it.' (Hadith Muslim 1791)

Religious living is deeply concerned with the doing of God's will, and this involves a ceaseless campaign against badness and the more subtle moral evils. Everybody knows it is wrong to steal, but not everyone cares about controlling spitefulness and envy. Evils like these spread outwards like a chain reaction.

They are like bad coins, which get passed from

one person to another until someone is generous enough to accept the loss himself or herself, and take the coin out of use.

If one person does something wrong to another, there are three ways in which evil can win a victory, and only one in which it can be defeated. The injured person could hit back in some way, or nurse a grudge, or take it out on someone else. In each of these cases, the evil is kept going and passed along. The evil is defeated only if the injured person is generous enough to 'take the coin out of use' - that is, to forgive the person who has caused offence, and not let the chain of evil go any further.

'Nor can goodness and evil be equal. Repel evil with what is better; then it will be that between whom and you was hatred will become as it were your friend and intimate.'
(Surah 41:34)

We must realise that God heals us as individuals from all those ills which hold us back from living a new life. Those ills may be of the soul - Allah heals by forgiving our sins, and enabling us to allow that forgiveness to flow out to others, and not least of all, to ourselves. He heals by mending hurtful memories, or anxiety caused by stress, irrational guilt, fear and all the psychological upsets which disturb our peace of mind.

We have to realise that God does not want us to suffer. He wants us to be healthy, happy and wholesome. Muslims learn to trust their lives to Allah, because they trust that ultimately everything is in His hands. The deepest form of healing will always be the forgiveness of sin, the putting right of our relationship with Him.

Some Muslims, unfortunately, look on the Creator-God as a Judge who is on the look-out to punish severely the tiniest fault, rather than as Supreme Compassion and Grace. Fear, not love, sin not grace, death not life, dominates their spiritual consciousness. Their religion is sometimes learned by rote from teachers, so that they may have all the answers to all the questions, but God has never become real for them in their hearts - even though they might win prizes for religious education!

Deep down, they are terrified about the state of their souls, believing themselves to be terrible people not worthy of God's mercy, and literally terrified of Hell. They have missed a very important part of Muslim understanding.

Abu Hurayrah reported: Allah, the Exalted the Glorious said: 'My mercy predominates over my anger.'   *(Hadith Muslim 6626)*

Yes, it is true that God approves and disapproves of certain things for which He has given clear guidelines in the Qur'an and which can also be deduced from the hadith. Yes, it is true that Muslims are guided by many rules and regulations of life and conduct - so many and comprehensive that it takes a life-time of dedication to know them all. But it is not true that any Muslim should take a superior stance over other people's apparent failings, or assume that any lapse from the 'straight path' will automatically land anyone in Hell. This is not what Islam teaches at all. If we just view life as a kind of pilgrimage in which we can earn good marks or bad as we journey towards a kind of examination, this presupposes that it is just to punish the wicked in Hell forever, even though this could not possibly have any function of reform. In other words, if the main purpose of punishment is to deter the evil-doer and bring reform, it is hard to see what place everlasting Hell could occupy in the plan of a good God. If the idea is simply that there must be an inexorable punishment to fit the crime, for what crime is an *everlasting* penalty a just one?

The real barriers to a healing closeness to God are arrogance and hostility. Arrogance, or pride, cannot yield its supremacy and domination to any person outside itself. Arrogant people put themselves out of reach of God's love, not because God ceases to love them, but because they are not receptive to that divine love which moves the universe.

There are some people whose very virtue stands in the way of the healing of their souls, because they feel resentment that God should have treated them so badly - they feel they deserve God's special providence because of their piety and work for His kingdom. We have to move beyond the thought of what we deserve, and how we should be rewarded. Until we become open to God's grace we simply block the power of His spirit to reach us, since He has granted us that freedom.

> *'Allah does not love that evil should be noised abroad in public speech, except where injustice has been done; for Allah is He who hears and knows all things. Whether you publish a good deed or conceal it, or cover evil with pardon - truly Allah blots out (sins) and has power.'*
> *(Surah 4:148-149)*

It is not for anyone to make 'righteous' assumptions about which of us are destined for Heaven or Hell. We have not the least knowledge about what God will decide, even for the worst of sinners.

> *'Not for you but for Allah is the decision, whether He turns in mercy to them or punishes them; for they are indeed wrongdoers.'*
> *(Surah 3:128)*

No matter what things may seem on the surface, no-one but God knows who has really accepted His offer in their hearts, and who rejected it. Only God can possibly know the destiny of any human spirit, and we are pretending to be God if we start declaring who is and who is not acceptable to Him. God cannot be bribed like a corrupt politician. If someone is suffering for some evil done to him, he may indeed try to make a contract with God, promising prayers and charitable deeds should the help needed arrive by God's will. Sometimes this kind of bargaining does seem to work - but it is not due to God particularly favouring that person. It is rather because the person has opened himself to receive God's spirit, in faith. As that faith grows, insha'Allah that person will cease to relate to God on the basis of bargaining; the feeling of closeness to God will be enough.

It is not God's purpose for any human being to end up in Hell. The only beings actually consigned to Hell are the Devil and His evil helpers. But if people use their God-given freewill to reject God's offer of forgiveness, then it may well be that they will share their terrible fate. If they do, it will not be God's choice, but theirs.

The kind of people we are talking about here are not those who fall short or fail in some detail of the high Islamic standards, but people who are literally *determined* to be evil and go against God. All the other sinners, the weak, those who have given in sometimes to temptation and then are sorry, the negligent, and so on - you and me - all are forgiven by God the moment they ask forgiveness.

> *'(Evil people will find their abode in Hell), except those who are (really) weak and oppressed, men, women and children, who have no means in their power, nor (a guide-post) to direct their way. For these, there is hope that Allah will forgive; for Allah blots out sins and forgives again and again.'*   *(Surah 4:98-99)*

And they will ask, because they are not of those who have denied God in their hearts. This does not excuse wrong behaviour, but it is important to realise that God's compassion is greater than any human person's.

Abu Musa reported Allah's Messenger (ﷺ) as saying that Allah, the Exalted and Glorious, stretches out His hand during the night so that the people repent for their faults committed from dawn to dusk, and He stretches out His hand during the day so that the people may repent for the fault committed from dusk to dawn.'   *(Hadith Muslim 6644)*

For those Muslims trapped upon the treadmill of trying to regulate every least detail of their lives in case they go to Hell, they cannot imagine God to be the Supremely Compassionate One, but see Him instead as a cruel and vindictive bully waiting to catch them out. They need an insight to give them a completely new way of thinking and acting - their fear of Allah is the wrong sort of fear.

Abu Hurayrah reported this beautiful hadith qudsi: *'I am near to the thought of My servant as he thinks about Me, and I am with him as he remembers Me. And if he remembers me in his heart, I also remember him in My heart.... and if he draws near Me by the span of a palm, I draw near him by the cubit, and if he walks towards Me, I run towards him.' (Hadith Muslim 6471)*

God is both Justice and Perfect Love. Those who refuse to meet Allah's conditions have good reason to fear Him; but those who have grown up in the atmosphere of His loving-kindness should know that there is no doubt that their repentance will be accepted. There can be nothing so heartbreaking to God as the spectacle of a person striving hard to serve Him in a callous and unbelieving society, actually believing he or she is in a danger of Hell fire because they simply forgot a prayer, or did it wrong, or said it at the wrong time!

Abu Hurayrah recorded: *'Whenever My servant intends to commit an evil, do not record it against him; but only if he actually commits it, then write it as one evil. And when he intends to do good, but does not do it, then take it down as one act of*

goodness; but if he does do it, then write down ten
good deeds.'   *(Hadith Muslim 233)*

It is tragic that some religious people feel that
they deserve to be punished because they do not
really love God as they should, and do not merit
His love. Yet God's love is completely unearned -
we can never merit it by our own unaided efforts. If
any Muslims have a sense of guilt to such an extent
that they feel God cannot forgive them completely,
this is wrong Islam. They say He is the Compassionate,
the Merciful, a hundred times per day, but they are
not believing it in their hearts. They fear God, and
stand in awe of His might, His power, His holiness
- but somehow the realisation of His love evades
them.

Abu Zubayr recorded: *'If he had in his heart*
virtue to the weight of one barley grain, he would
come out of the Fire.'   *(Hadith Muslim 367)*

Anas b. Malik recorded: *'He would bring out of*
the Fire anyone who professed: 'There is no God
but Allah', even though that person had in his or
her heart virtue (only) equal to the weight of one
atom.'   *(Hadith Muslim 376)*

True Faith brings us to God and does not drive us
away. The motivating force of those whose life is
based on love for God, is not fear or obligation. No-

one who knows God can fear Him any longer in that sense. They lose the need for an ulterior motive - all they wish to do is offer themselves humbly, in loving service to Him and all He has created, and to venture forth in His world in the power of that love. It may be that the over-strict religious zealot becomes like that because that person has never known the real human love of a father. One finds deep inner damage in people who suffer from an unhappy childhood where they were the victims of selfish, demanding possessive parents - no matter how 'religious' they might have claimed to be. These people often grow up hating themselves, and because of their inner feelings of resentment towards their parents, they are unable to relate to Allah as a God of Love and Mercy, Al-Rahman, Al-Rahim.

Here is a beautiful story from the hadith to illustrate the mercy of Allah:

Abu Said al-Khudri recorded: 'There was a person before you who killed ninety-nine persons,.... and asked whether there was any scope for his repentance to be accepted.... He said: 'Yes. What stands between you and the repentance? Go to such and such a land; there you will find people devoted to worship and prayer, so you may also worship along with them.'.. He had covered half the distance when death came upon him, and there was a dispute between the angels of mercy and the angels of punishment. The angels of mercy said; 'This man has come as a penitent and is remorseful to Allah'; and the angels of punishment said: 'He has done no good at all.' Then there came another angel in the form of a human being, to decide between them. He said: 'Measure the distance to the land to which he was drawing near.' Allah realised he had not travelled far enough, and so He moved the entire earth on that repentant sinner's behalf. When the angels measured the distance, they found him nearer to the land where he intended to go, and so the angels of mercy took possession of him. Qatada said that Hasan told him that it was said to them that as death approached him, he crawled upon his chest to slip into the land of mercy.'   *(Hadith Muslim 6662)*

The false attitude to forgiveness which sees God only as a vengeful Judge has done untold damage over the centuries. When we make fear of punishment in this life and the next the chief motive in religion, it means that the soul is so shrivelled, the mind so tormented, and the body so suppressed, that Allah cannot 'unlock the door' of our hearts, bolted by fear, which we can only open from the inside. We need true faith to set us free.

Abu Dharr recorded that the Apostle (ﷺ) observed: 'Jibril came to me and told me the tidings - Truly, he who died amongst your Ummah without associating anything with Allah would enter Paradise.' I said: 'Even if he committed adultery and theft?' He (the Holy Prophet) (ﷺ) said: 'Yes, even if he committed adultery and theft.' (Hadith Muslim 171 - this hadith, incidentally supports the viewpoint of the Ahl-i-Sunnah that, except kufr and shirk, no misdeed, however serious, dooms a human being to eternal Fire).

Fear and guilt can so permeate people's lives that no amount of preaching or study of the love and forgiveness in the Holy Text can get through to them. These are the very types who form cliques and become sectarians, and who regard others who do not share their opinions or regimes to be less good Muslims than themselves.

CHAPTER NINE

LOVE OF ALLAH

It is love of Allah which unblocks the coldness, bitterness, the ache of bereavement, the pain of loneliness and rejection, the resentment at our ill-treatment by others, and the thousand other things that keeps us so locked up we are unable to love even ourselves. Once we believe in our hearts that He loves us and wants us whole, and takes no pleasure whatsoever in the thought that by our own stupidity and perversity we might end up in Hell - then we remove from our lives the obstacle of fear which destroys our trust in Him. He loves us all individually, even to our fingerprints. He knows us better than we know ourselves.

Sadly, not every Muslim remains true to their calling - too many are led by Shaytan down the road of self-righteousness and exclusiveness. The self-righteous virtuous often feel threatened by the real compassion of true Islam. Outer moral rectitude can often be devoid of compassion for the pariahs of society. A morality without love soon deteriorates into a zeal for condemnation and persecution. Evil actual flourishes best in such a milieu, because it can hide behind the bastions of propriety and religion, and even claim to be acting on behalf of God.

Real Islam does not see any person as being evil, but as infected by evil. Each individual is a 'child' of Allah and a brother or sister who has fallen into fearful trouble.

God's love is not conditional - as if He will only love us if we do this or that; God's love for us does not ebb and flow - it is unchangeable. It is *our* love, and our response that is fickle; and it is a tragedy that so many Muslims feel that because they may have done something which estranged them temporarily from God, that He has in consequence distanced Himself from them. This is not true - God never ceases to love us, no matter what we have done. We have only to turn back and be sorry, and His forgiveness overflows. But God never forces Himself upon the person who needs Him. He waits to be approached. He does not invade their personality or wear down their will. If an individual steadfastly refuses to confront the corruption within, or simply rationalises it away, he or she will remain in bondage to it. If we cling to past attitudes we remain subject to all their limitations and constraints. But when we do call upon God, and implore His keep and mercy,

He immediately takes control of the situation, and will never let go. God is never nearer to us than in our times of emergency.

God's love is unchanging even when *we* change for the worse and forget Him. Even though we may think we are worthless, God thinks the opposite, especially when we have no-one to love us, not even ourselves! He never ceases to love us. When we sin, it is we, and not God, who put up the barriers. It is not true that we have to spend the rest of our lives in penitential acts and prayers, trying desperately to appease Him and 'soften Him up' - that is the sin of despair, and not trusting God. We do not have to spend our time repeatedly chanting various phrases and prayers in a desperate attempt to clock up points of merit. That time would no doubt be far better spent genuinely apologizing to Allah for what we have done wrong, or omitted to do right, and then to go forth and seek practical and compassionate ways of serving Him by being a good khalifah to His created ones and beloved planet.

Those who stress the wickedness of sin without emphasizing also the limitless mercy and forgiveness of a loving God do a grave disservice to Islam. They are trapped in a bog of self-condemnation, and are trying to limit the mercy of God to their own narrow dimensions. They are not building up repentance but a whole load of neuroses in those they should be helping.

These Muslims are so slavishly afraid of Allah that they are afraid to love Him. Fear is basically a lack of faith and hope. People who live in fear of God do not really believe deep down that He has the power to help them or change them; or maybe they think that He does have the power, but doesn't care anyway. Fear of failure soon gives rise to depression and anxiety - but faith and hope give us courage to face up to ourselves and to life. What God says to us is much more important than what we say to Him.

The Qur'an and hadiths teach us how to love God, our neighbours and ourselves in the way Allah wants us to; and the deepening of this capacity to love is a continuing, never-ending process. In order to love others, and to respect them as that love requires, we must recognise their special relationship with God. Things are never quite as they seem to us. We think that we know everything, that we know best. This is far from being the case.

God calls each individual and puts the desire to be accepted by Him in his or her heart - but before we can recognise this in others, we must find it in ourselves. We have to experience the faithfulness of Allah towards us, no matter now unfaithful to Him we have been! If we wish to see our neighbours as we should, we should try to see them through the 'eyes of God'. Only then can we truly love them. This is why it is also necessary to see ourselves through the 'eyes of God'. To bear witness to Allah and to help others to know Him and come to Him, we need to live with Him and stay with Him. This is what we call taqwa, or God-consciousness. This is why we accept the discipline of the five pillars, and try to come closer to God's mystery and love by it.

You may have had a good Muslim upbringing in a good home and mosque. But what you have heard and observed is useless to you unless you believe it and act on it for yourself. No-one can do this for you, on your behalf, because each one of us has to make his or her own response to God - first hand. We cannot be 'second hand' Muslims.

If you feel lonely, or isolated, your prayer is the end to your isolation. It means living our daily life with Someone. He is the only One we can find in our own heart, closer to us than our own jugular vein, to Whom we can tell anything that is in us. He, of course, is always present, even if we do not realise it. Our prayer hopefully makes us aware of His presence, which we might not realise if we did not pay attention.

It is the living Presence of Him who knows everything about us, and from Whom we receive everything. That is why we should be humble - not because we want to concentrate on our weakness or helplessness or poor talents, but a joyful humility because He is so great and yet so close to us. It does not matter if we are 'nobody', if we have 'nothing' - our love for Allah is a love which gives us everything. We 'know' God by being aware of Him in ourselves, surrounding us, guiding our lives. Our prayer is the acceptance of Someone Who has a plan for us.

Even if our faith is small and incomplete, we can grasp as much as we can of it, and live by it through all manner of adversity and trials. Allah allows us to guess and glimpse His will, and our faith in Him becomes our support. Even when everything seems empty, we can be certain that Allah is there. He cannot fail us, however badly we fail. If we live simply with this certainty, we will realise more and more the truth of His Presence and we will feel the joy.

The meaning of our time of trial here is not selfish, (the impression given by some Muslims of limited insight); it is not just to give us the chance to earn a reward in the Hereafter. It is to teach us how to love, to enable us to enter into a true loving relationship with Allah. If Allah sometimes keeps us in the dark, this is not because He wishes to hurt or confuse us, but it is in order to lead us to a deeper communion with Him through the lessons we learn. We have to put our whole selves into the hands of Him who is our only reason for living.

Life is given to us to learn to believe. We are, hopefully, heading towards Heaven. If we believe that we will have existence as individuals in that Heaven, then what we mean by individual existence is based on the notions and ideas of this world. What do we mean by 'us'? 'We' are beings who recognise ourselves as individuals in space and time. There would be no 'us' if we had been predestined for Heaven and placed there straight away without going through all the ups and downs of human experience.

Everything that happens, no matter how upsetting, should lead us further in our faith. When things go wrong for us, and we get hurt, these are the very times when we begin to see our way most clearly. How? Well, whatever our difficulties and our fears of going astray, we can be sure that we are on the Straight Path if what happens to us teaches us to understand more and more clearly what it means to have faith. We belong to Allah, we are in His hands. This is the ground of all our hope, and nothing can destroy this because it is beyond earthly hope.

We should be amazed that Allah loves us, and never be fooled into thinking that His love could fail us. We should have the humility to see that our wretchedness, however, great, cannot be an obstacle to the power of God. It doesn't matter if we don't understand everything. If we truly believe in Him, if He truly means everything to us, we have only to turn in His direction. We should offer ourselves to Him in all our weakness and insecurity with nothing but our desire to obey Him and let Him work in us.

If we cannot express ourselves properly, it doesn't matter. Allah knows what we are trying to say, and trying to do. To be Muslim means 'to submit', 'to accept'. We must accept our trials and difficulties, even upsetting ones, even ones which come from other people, perhaps from those we love. We must accept everything and everybody Allah uses to fulfil His plan for us. When it is impossible for us not to be sad, our sadness should still have the serenity of faith. We must accept suffering and not become bitter.

We must not worry about all that is human and weak in us - Allah, our Creator, knows all about it, and still loves us - but we must learn to recognise His Presence in the midst of our difficulties and trials. We must have confidence in Him. When someone makes us suffer, we should not hate them, for this is an unworthy attitude, but should try to discover how to behave in such a way as to help our tormentor to improve. Because, we have to remember that God loves that person too.

We must not be hostile, or superior, or quick to judge and censor others. Humility towards God in accepting the trials He sends us must be part of our deepest beings. Sometimes the great barrier to forgiveness is not a crippling awareness of guilt, but our overweening sense of self-righteousness that is made rigid in resentment. As soon as we can give up our self-righteous stance and gaze with compassion at the creatures around us - including those who have injured us - then we can see our own need for forgiveness no less than theirs. We Muslims can at least prostrate ourselves in true humility and awareness of Allah's compassion, whereas those who have abused us may well remain in dark ignorance about themselves and what the future life has in store for them.

Once we have mastered our resentment, our thoughts can be transfigured by God's forgiveness, into love. We will no longer need to seek justice, let alone revenge. We can turn our thoughts and gaze to those who have wronged us, and try to be the instruments of their forgiveness also.

Love works unremittingly for the redemption of all that is imprisoned in hatred, terror and ignorance, all that is perverse, unclean and imprisoned in chains of resentment and fear. Love can never rest until all God's creatures are free to receive the life-giving power He wishes to bestow upon us.

Let us believe in God's love, in His faithfulness. He is always at work in our hearts, He never slumbers nor sleeps. His grace takes hold of every heart that really desires it, however poor and weak that heart may feel.

We cannot see God, but we can welcome the gift of His Presence. His Presence begins our awareness, and opens the way to His love. That love remains with us, even when we cannot feel it, even in the dark times when we have doubts.

If Allah is Who the Qur'an says He is, and if our Creator is trying to communicate with us, then if we do not respond we are missing the whole purpose of our existence. Allah has spoken, so we must answer.

What kind of people does Allah love? He loves us, while we are still sinners, while we are still powerless and helpless, while we are still ungrateful. And He loves them, while they are still sinners, ungrateful, and maybe nasty to us. He knows things we do not know; He sees what we do not see. He sees their hearts, and knows the reasons why they behave as they do; He sees your heart, and knows how you cope with their hostility.

Remember, Allah hates no person that He has made, but He hates sin and evil! He cannot tolerate, excuse or condone it. He asks you, if you love Him, to be His warriors against all sin and injustice, wherever you may find it - but not to hate His created beings. You may love this person more than that person, because you are human - but Allah does not love in our way, He loves without limits.

His compassion, His generosity, His freedom has no limits - He loves every person, even the ones you do not like or disapprove of. The pitiful, unpleasant, selfish, unkind, spiteful dishonest person is also loved by Allah - indeed, maybe those kind of people are so revolting that Allah is the only One who can love them, even if, sadly, the punishment they draw on themselves is their ultimate end.

We have thought in all these pages about all sorts of aspects of what people believe. Now we have come to the end, it is important to realise that no two people ever really believe the same things about God. He probably doesn't mind this in the least, or He wouldn't have provided us with brains to think things out, and often to come to the wrong conclusions. What was important to the Blessed Messengers of God should be important to us, and that was not a desperate attempt to work out subtle problems that were far too deep for us; on the contrary, it was that we should be loving, forgiving, unselfish, generous people. That is what would make anyone say of you - 'that person is a real Muslim.'